BIG DATA

IMPLEMENTATION

Prof. Marcão - Marcus Vinícius Pinto

Disclaimer:

Please note that the information contained in this document is for educational and entertainment purposes only. Every effort has been made to provide complete, accurate, up-to-date and reliable information. No warranty of any kind is express or implied.

By reading this text, the reader agrees that under no circumstances are the authors liable for any losses, direct or indirect, incurred as a result of the use of the information contained in this book, including, but not limited to, errors, omissions, or inaccuracies.

ISBN: 9798880004522

Selo editorial: Independently published

To my beloved Andrea.

More than a peerless wife and companion,

an inspiration at all times.

"You can have data without information, but you cannot have information without data."

Daniel Keys Moran[1]

---

[1] Daniel Keys Moran has worked on some of the largest websites in the world. He coined the word "webcast" and is the author of "The Tales of the Continuing Time," a series that Wikipedia describes as containing "multiple universes, time travel, cyberpunk, alien invasions, martial arts, dance, and paganism.

Welcome.

In today's business world, effective implementation of Big Data has become an essential element in driving success and competitiveness. As organizations dive into the vast sea of data available, the ability to extract meaningful and actionable insights has become a crucial differentiator for driving successful strategies and achieving ambitious goals.

This book highlights the importance of continuous improvement in the use of Big Data, emphasizing that the data analysis process is inherently iterative and demands a mindset focused on the relentless pursuit of improvements and innovations.

The following pages cover the various dimensions of Big Data implementation, from setting clear objectives to selecting appropriate technologies, collecting and integrating data, analyzing and extracting insights, visualizing and communicating results, to monitoring and making necessary adjustments. Each chapter offers valuable insights and practical guidance to guide organizations towards an efficient and strategic use of Big Data.

At the heart of this approach is the premise that organizations must be prepared to embrace constant change by adopting new technologies, strengthening the skills of their teams, and adapting quickly to changing market and consumer demands.

The relentless pursuit of continuous improvement not only provides a significant competitive advantage, but also opens doors to innovation, process optimization, and maximizing the value derived from Big Data.

As we move forward in this exciting field of data analytics and Big Data, this book serves as a trusted guide for organizations looking to effectively integrate these technologies into their operations and strategies. Be prepared to embark on a journey of discovery, learning, and most of all, transformation. The future of business is being shaped by the insights generated from data analytics and the ability to adapt to continuous change and innovation.

By remaining agile and responsive to transformations in the business and technology landscape, organizations can not only stand out in a competitive environment but also redefine standards for excellence and leadership in their respective industries.

In this book, I invite you to explore every aspect of Big Data implementation with critical eyes and an open mind, ready to absorb valuable knowledge and insightful insights that will shape your understanding and practice of data analytics in an information-driven world. By incorporating the principles of continuous improvement into your big data approach, you'll be paving the way for success and innovation on your journey to analytics excellence.

Get ready for a deep dive into the fascinating universe of Big Data and data analytics. Not only does this book offer a comprehensive and practical guide to effectively implementing Big Data in your organization, but it also inspires you to embrace the constant improvement mindset that is essential for leveraging the transformative potential of data analytics.

Taking Facebook, for example, it generates 64 TB of data per day. Companies like Google, Amazon, and Yahoo are on the same level and major companies around the world will soon reach this same volume.

Not to mention the variety of data generated: social networks, server logs, email, data from ERP and CRM systems, monitoring cameras, sensors. The following figure presents the terminology of the number of bytes that have become part of IT when it comes to the amount of data trafficked on the Internet.

To enter this world and work as a Big Data expert, you will need to develop the ability to design, deploy, and utilize the infrastructure required for processing large databases.

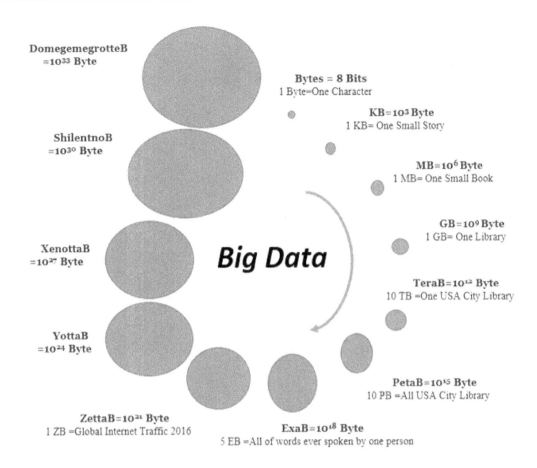

Figure 1 – The terminology of byte quantities.

The following figure illustrates the complexity of the Big Data universe by presenting what is proper to Big Data and what is around it. In this book we will deal with the topics that are essential for the knowledge of Big Data.

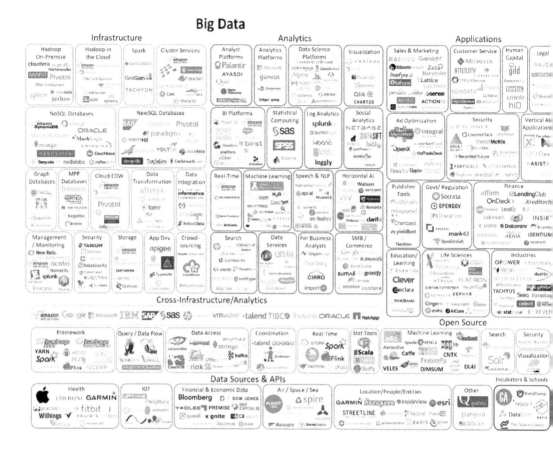

Figure 2 – Universo de Big Data.

This processing may involve *cloud computing*, proprietary servers or hybrid environments. There is also a need to know new technologies, such as Hadoop and NoSQL databases.

The professional in this segment also needs to be able to apply artificial intelligence algorithms to create prediction models.

Data is changing our world and the way we live and work in an unprecedented way. Depending on your point of view, we're either at the beginning of something incredibly exciting or we're entering the terrifying era of Big Brother where our every move can be tracked and even predicted.

Business leaders and managers, however, have little time for data skepticism. Data is already revolutionizing the way businesses operate and will become increasingly critical to businesses in the coming years.

Figure 3 – New Big Data tools.

Companies that see data as a strategic asset are the ones that will survive and thrive for the foreseeable future. With the massive growth of Big Data and the Internet of Things, as well as the rapid evolution of methods for data analysis, the importance of data in all areas of business will only grow.

Data science, on the other hand, is an emerging field. Demand is high, and finding qualified personnel is one of the main challenges associated with Big Data analytics.

A data scientist may be based in IT or in the business – but wherever he or she is, he or she will be your new best friend and collaborator in the planning and implementation of big data analytics projects (Davenport et al., 2012).

Big data is a tsunami on the high seas, and it's already coming to trample everything we know. Therefore, I suggest starting to study and understand the subject better. Being prepared is improving employability!

Here, I tried to bring, in a single volume, complete information, concepts and resources necessary for the profession and best practices for you to be an excellent professional.

I recommend this book to students and professionals of Information Science, Information Technology, Computing and other professionals who aspire to perform functions in the field of information technology.

I am excited to share this journey with you and to witness the extraordinary achievements that will be achieved through the strategic and innovative application of Big Data. Together, we will explore new horizons and achieve new heights of success in a world driven by data analytics and the relentless pursuit of excellence.

The future is bright – and the key to unlocking its full potential is in your hands. Onward, towards a new era of opportunities and achievements!

Happy reading!
Happy studying!
Happy data analysis!
Be part of the Big Data world!
Prof. Marcão – Marcus Pinto

Summary

Index of Figures

*"Data is the new science.
Big data holds the answers."*

Patrick Paul Gelsinger

1   O BIG DATA.

IT professionals are used to dealing with databases with different structures, different manipulation languages, and different communication networks. However, each architecture has its application and constitutes a solution to a certain class of problems, dealing with certain data sources.

In the ever-expanding world of the internet, we are faced with a plethora of data sources that need to be properly managed, researched, and analyzed to serve a variety of specific purposes.

However, as the amount and variety of this data grows exponentially, the problem of effectively managing it becomes increasingly complex, challenging, and in many cases, seemingly impossible to scale.

What once could be a promising solution for gaining valuable insights and information quickly turns into a huge obstacle that requires a nuanced approach and innovative strategies.

Big data management, in this context, becomes a pressing need for businesses, organizations, and even individuals looking to benefit from the vast resources available.

Collecting, storing, processing, and analyzing these massive volumes of data require specialized technologies and infrastructures that can handle the demands of scale and complexity.

Distributed database management systems, cloud storage, and distributed processing platforms are just a few examples of technologies that have emerged to respond to these challenges.

In addition to the technological infrastructure, it is also important to consider the aspects related to data governance in this context. The quality of the data, its security, and regulatory compliance are crucial factors to address. It is necessary to establish sound data governance policies and practices to ensure the integrity, privacy, and confidentiality of the information handled. Protecting against cyber threats, complying with data protection laws, and mitigating algorithmic bias are just a few of the ethical and legal concerns that need to be considered.

Effectively understanding and analyzing data is also one of the main challenges. Advanced statistical methods, machine learning, data mining, and data visualization are essential techniques that can be applied in big data analytics. By extracting meaningful and relevant insights from this voluminous and complex data, organizations can make informed and strategic decisions, driving innovation, operational efficiency, and business success.

In addition, the practical application of big data spans diverse industries and has numerous use cases. Data analytics can be used to improve the effectiveness of sales and marketing strategies, develop more personalized healthcare solutions, optimize transportation and logistics systems, monitor financial activities, and improve governance in public entities. Each industry has its own specific needs and goals, and proper big data management plays a key role in each of these contexts.

However, in the face of the growing volume of data and the consequent ethical and social implications, it is essential to address broader issues related to the responsible and ethical use of big data. This includes ensuring transparency in the collection and use of data, protecting the privacy and rights of individuals, avoiding discrimination and unfair algorithmic bias, and ensuring that the benefits of big data are distributed equitably.

Thus, we can say that being faced with so much data, with so many varied forms, it is impossible to think of a "traditional" management. New challenges call for new solutions. Big Data is "the" new solution.

It is possible to think of the evolution of data management as isolated stages of technological advancement. According to Stonebraker (2012), these stages are not necessarily an evolution of the previous stage. However, whether unpublished or derivative, most of the technological advances of the stages are based on their precursors.

Although the advances in DBMS[2] and data architecture management approaches are seen as the evolutionary foundations of the information world, it is necessary to understand this evolution in the context of software + hardware + data. According to Hilbert (2013):

> *"Technological revolutions combined with cost reductions, considering scenarios of reduction in the size of storage devices with a large increase in the volume of data recorded and high gains in computational processing speed, have made it possible to develop new perspectives and the emergence of opportunities in the universe of the intersection of platforms and data sources, generating new management products."*

As all of these technology factors converge, we are experiencing a complete transformation in the way we manage and use data. Big Data is the latest trend to emerge from all of these factors.

It is defined as any type of data analytics platform that has these five characteristics:

- Extremely large volumes.

- Technological architecture with extremely high processing speed capability.

- Wide range of data types processed.

- Data with potential value for the company

- Data with high reliability.

1.1   5 Vs do Big Data.

Big Data experts have developed a theory called the 5 Vs (Subramaniam, 2020). The

---

[2] Database Management Systems - DBMS is a software for database management, which allows you to create, modify and insert elements. The term originates from the English Data Base Management System, or simply DBMS.

following figure illustrates this theory.

Figure 4 – Os 5Vs do Big Data

- Volume.

  - The concept of volume in Big Data is evidenced by internet traffic made up of email exchanges, banking transactions, interactions on social networks, call logs, and data traffic on telephone lines.

  - It is estimated that the total volume of data circulating on the internet in 2021 is 340 Exabytes per year.

  - Every day 2.9 quintillion bytes are created in the form of data, currently 90% of all data that is present in the world was created in the last 3 years (Manyika (2011)).

- It is also important to understand that the concept of volume is a variable that depends on the time considered, that is, what is great today, may be nothing tomorrow. (Lohr, 2012) (Ohlhorst, 2012).

- In the 1990s, a Terabyte (1012 bytes) was considered Big Data.

- Speed.

   - Would you cross a street blindfolded if the last information you had was a photograph taken of the traffic 5 minutes ago? Probably not, as the photo from 5 minutes ago is irrelevant now. You need to know the current conditions so that you can cross the street safely. (Forbes, 2012). The same logic applies to companies, as they need current data about their business, i.e., speed.

   - According to Taurion (2013), the importance of speed is such that at some point there must be a tool capable of analyzing the data in real time.

   - Currently, data is analyzed only after it is stored, but the time taken for storage itself already disqualifies this type of analysis as a 100% real-time analysis.

   - Information is power (Rogers, 2010), and therefore, the speed with which this information is obtained is a competitive advantage for companies.

   - Speed can limit the operation of many businesses, when we use the credit card, for example, if we do not get an approval of the purchase in a few seconds we usually think about using another payment method. It's the operator missing out on a business opportunity due to the failure to speed up transmission and analyze the buyer's data.

   - Daily and long-term analysis of Big Data can be done. Both cases can be useful for the person responsible for this area to know how to identify the speed with which the analyses need to be done.

- Variety.

  - Volume is just the beginning of the challenges of this new technology, if we have a huge volume of data, we also have a huge variety of it.

  - Have you ever thought about the amount of information scattered on social networks? Facebook, Twitter, among others, have a vast and distinct field of information being offered in public every second.

  - We can observe the variety of data in emails, social networks, photographs, audios, phones and credit cards. (McAffe et al, 2012). We can get infinite points of view on the same information.

  - Companies that can capture variety, whether in sources or criteria, add more value to the business.

  - Big Data scales the variety of information in the following ways:

    o Structured data: This is stored in databases, sequenced in tables. Example: tables or forms filled out by customers.

    o Semi-structured data: they follow heterogeneous patterns, they are more difficult to identify because they can follow different patterns. For example, if an image is taken from a smartphone, it will have some structured attributes like geotag, device ID, and timestamp. Once stored, images can also be tagged as 'pet' or 'dog' to provide a structure.

    o Unstructured data: This is a mixture of data with diverse sources such as images, audios, and online documents. Example: messages, photos, videos.

  - Among these 3 categories, it is estimated that up to 90% of all data in the world is in the form of unstructured data.

- Truthfulness.

  - One in 3 leaders do not trust the data they receive (IBM, 2014).

  - To reap good results from the Big Data process, it is necessary to obtain truthful data, according to reality.

  - The concept of speed, already analyzed, is linked to the concept of veracity by the constant need for real-time analysis. This means that the data matches the reality at that moment, because past data cannot be considered true data for the later moment.

  - The relevance of the data collected is as important as the volume, as there is no point in having quantity without quality.

  - The verification of the collected data for adequacy and relevance to the purpose of the analysis is a key point to obtain data that adds value to the process.

  - Not all of the data collected is true. This is the case, for example, with fake news3, which can spread quickly on the Internet.

- Value.

  - It is necessary to focus on the orientation of the business, as the value of collecting and analyzing the data is measured by the benefit it will bring to the business.

  - It is not feasible to carry out the entire Big Data process if you do not have questions that help the business in a realistic way.

---

3 Fake news is fake news published by media outlets as if it were real information. In evidence since 2016, its popularization was due to the US elections that defined Donald Trump as the 45th president of the United States.

- In the same way, it is important to be aware of the costs involved in this operation, the added value of all this work developed, collection, storage and analysis of all this data has to compensate for the financial costs involved (Taurion, 2013).

- The information can have special value for a company's marketing campaigns. The idea is for the team to evaluate which data is more or less valuable and apply it to their strategies according to their degree of importance.

As you can see, Big Data is indispensable for success and improvements in several areas of your company. It should be seen as a kind of compass that every entrepreneur should use to get to know themselves, their audience, and their competition.

Big Data is important because it provides a means for the company to store, manage, and process large amounts of data according to its needs (Glass et al. (2015). But realize that it is important to keep in mind that Big Data is the result of the evolution of data management and it is essential to understand how the last 50 years of technology maturation determined the emergence of this new technology.

Companies have been experiencing a multitude of problems in their data management for some time now, as they have evolved from the stage where DW technology was quite sufficient.

Today, companies are dealing with more data from more sources than previously thought possible. All of this data is known as "the new oil," but without the proper tools, drilling for this "oil" does not produce wealth.

In these new times, the challenges of data management technology are:

1. How does the company work with huge amounts of data in a way that considers it as a useful collection?

2. How can we make sense of this immensity of data if it is not possible to

recognize the patterns to make them meaningful for the company's business processes and decisions?

1.2   The concept of Big Data.

To get a sense of the evolution of something, it is necessary to identify significant differences between the results of the various versions of that something. For example, when we talk about the evolution of automobiles, we have distinct phases, starting with animal-drawn vehicles, evolving to steam automobiles, moving on to simple combustion engines, arriving at the current electric autonomous vehicles. It is easy to understand the different stages of the automotive product.

Figure 5 – Too much data?

Data management is no different. Taking as a focus of validating the difference between the generations of managers the way to solve the problems posed then, it is possible to affirm that each generation evolved due to cause and effect factors.

When a new technology hits the market, it establishes new ways of working. A good example was the arrival on the market of relational database technology. Due to the huge differences between this proposal and previous solutions, it was necessary for companies to look for ways to adapt to make good use of their resources.

The previous generation, dominated by[4] IBM's[5] VSAM, was quickly abandoned due to the potential for processing much larger databases and more modular and versatile programs.

The technological generation based on object orientation was faced with new forms of programming, but there was no real evolution in the management of databases.

A new scenario was posed by the storage of unstructured data in which it was necessary for information technology professionals to become familiar with natural language-based analysis tools to generate useful results for the companies' businesses.

At the same time, the evolution of search engines has given rise to tools that aimed to generate profit from the indexing and retrieval of significant data in the internet scenario.

This evolutionary process that began before the turn of the century culminated where we are with the arrival of Big Data. An essential characteristic of this

---

[4] VIRTUAL STORAGE ACCESS METHOD - VSAM. The Virtual Storage Access Method. It is a file management method that is primarily used on mainframes, but also on PCs. VSAM accelerates access to file data by using a reverse index of records attached to files. This index is called the B+ tree.

[5] International Business Machines Corporation (IBM) is an American computer company. IBM manufactures and sells hardware and software, offers infrastructure services, hosting services, and consulting services in areas ranging from large computers to nanotechnology. It was nicknamed "Big Blue" for adopting blue as its official corporate color, in Portuguese "Big Blue".

evolutionary process is the fact that from one generation to another there was no substitution of tools, methodologies and concepts, but rather the generation of a range of alternatives for different problems. Big Data is a derivative of this range of solutions.

Returning to the context of technology in the mid-1960s, when computing presented itself as a processing alternative in the commercial enterprise market, data were stored in simple files, magnetic tapes, which had primary structures.

When companies needed more complex outcomes to support their decision-making processes or their production and product delivery chain, it took a superhuman effort to create value from those files.

As early as the 1970s, Peter Chen revolutionized data managers by proposing the relational data model that imposed a new structure and aimed at improving computer parks.

However, the main differential of this approach was the introduction of abstraction levels through the structured query language, SQL, [6]and report generators.

The relational model, enhanced by Charles Bachman and James Martin, consolidated a way of thinking, working and processing data that met the growing needs of companies that, at this time, were present in several countries, becoming transnational.

This technology has allowed business managers to examine stratified, segmented, and cross-referenced information such as the number of items in inventories

---

[6] SQL stands for "Structured Query Language" Portuguese which stands for Structured Query Language, a standard data management language that interacts with major databases based on the relational model. Some of the main systems that use SQL are: MySQL, Oracle, Firebird, Microsoft Access, PostgreSQL (open source), HSQLDB (open source and written in Java).

distributed relative to the quantities of regionalized orders and customer profiles segmented by income class that would have been impossible with previous generations of database managers.

Figure 6 – Charles Bachman e James Martin.

But this beautiful scenery brought with it a new problem. How do you store this growing volume of data? Storage was getting more and more expensive, and processing was getting slower and slower. As a consequence, it was difficult to assess whether all this infrastructure had real value for companies.

Despite the weaknesses of the entity-relationship model, it has established itself as a data management standard for transactional systems based on highly structured data.

However, the problem of processing managerial and strategic information increased every day. The growth in the volume of data that companies needed to process reached an unchecked level by the end of the 1990s.

It was then that William H. Inmon (Inmon, 1992,1996) presented his definition of DW that provided a solution characterized by:

- Guidance by subject. DW's data structure modeling orientation is oriented towards the core issues of the company, while transactional systems are focused on transactional processes and applications.

- Integration. All data created in the DW environment is created in subject segments, the data marts,[7] which are integrated forming a base in which all data is integrated. Integration is made possible by adopting the following guidelines:

  o Attribute names are standardized.

  o The comments of the attributes are designed according to the whole of the company and not to a specific information system.

  o The information is encoded according to standards adopted by all the company's information systems.

  o The types, sizes and formats of attributes are standardized and adopted in all company databases

- Variance in time. While in transactional systems databases maintain data according to the processes in which they are used, in DW the data timeline is maintained without interruption, as its main objective is to analyze the behavior of data over a longer period.

- Non-volatity. In DW there are only two operations: data loading and data queries. In this structure, the data is periodically copied from the transactional database. No change or deletion, allowing you to derive the multidimensional

---

[7] Data Mart - It is a small data warehouse, covering a certain subject area and offering more detailed information about the market (or department) in question. A set of a company's data marts make up the data warehouse.

data model.

For a better understanding of this approach, let's take the example of a cruise liner company. Using a DW it is possible to obtain information based on the historical series of the ships' voyages. It is possible to identify in which region of the world there is the greatest demand for a particular cruise at a given time of the year (Kimball et al., 2013). It is also possible to expand the detail of this query by identifying the origin of these passengers.

The following figure presents an infographic with some of the complexity of the analysis of cruise ships.

With this information in a timely manner, that is, at the end of the cruise season, it is possible for managers to plan the cruise calendar for the next season offering advantages to passengers in a certain region of the world.

The same example applies to social programs in which it is possible for public managers to base their actions according to the historical analysis of a given subject. For example, with public school enrollment data, it would be possible, through the analysis of the historical series of student results, to identify in which region there are higher school dropouts and to act on the maintenance of students in the classrooms.

Improvements in virtualization technologies and improvements in hardware scalability have brought many benefits and broadened the fields of action for database managers and data warehouses. At the same time, the increase in the performance of data marts was another factor in the expansion of the use of Data Warehouses.

Data marts had their use expanded by focusing on specific problems of the company's business, responding to quick queries, behaving as small DWs that, as they had their use approved, were incorporated into the corporate DW.

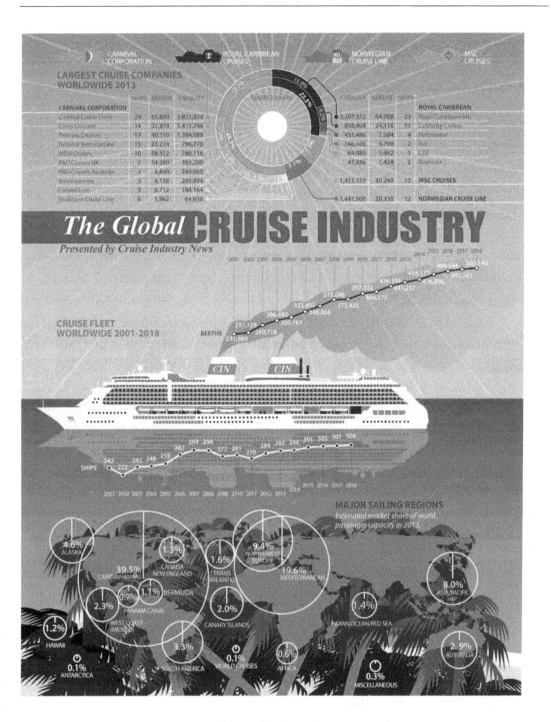

Figure 7– Infographic based on cruise ships.

The DW + data mart suite solved many managerial and strategic data generation problems, but proved inadequate to address problems that needed to process unstructured or semi-structured data.

One of the reasons for this inadequacy to the new processing demands is precisely one of the pillars of the Data Warehouse. Its structure is based on periodic loads that serve well the initial purpose of generating data for planning, financial reporting and traditional marketing campaigns, but it is too slow for companies and consumers who need real-time analysis and results.

It should be noted here that unstructured content cannot be treated in conventional attributes in relational databases. As a solution to store them in the databases, so that they would not be lost, the unstructured data was stored contiguous blocks of data, in fields such as BLOBs – *Binary Large* Object. This type of field was created for the storage of any type of information in binary format, within a table of a relational database.

Although very useful for storing unstructured data, this type of field does not allow its content to be used in processing because it was not possible to know what was inside it. The BLOB was widely used, then, for image storage.

In the current scenario, in which most of the data available in the world is unstructured, there is a new market, with disconnected solutions that have evolved into unified business process management platforms.

This new platform of solutions incorporated metadata such as information about the company's performance and characteristics of the information stored about this performance.

At the same time, requirements engineering has been faced with a new generation of specifications that is based on the convergence of the web with virtualization, cloud computing, and big data.

These new requirements reflect the demands of companies that are beginning to incorporate into their work process the need to manage a new generation of data sources with unprecedented quantities and varieties that need to be processed and generate useful results at a speed never seen before.

The evolution of data managers then reaches the current technological proposal, Big Data. And there we have a very present issue in the companies' analyses. Is Big Data really something new in the world of data processing, or is it a natural evolution of technology?

Although it may seem incoherent to say that it is the result of the natural evolution of data management and something entirely new, this is the answer (Helbing, 2015a). While it builds on everything that has gone before in data management, it introduces fundamental innovations by solving problems such as the cost of compute cycles, the increasing complexity of storage, and the management of huge databases.

Big Data makes it possible to virtualize data so that it can be stored more efficiently and more cost-effectively using cloud-based storage.

At the same time, the new data processing landscape has at its disposal improvements in the speed and reliability of networks, changes in prices and in the sophistication of computer memory.

And, finally, after so many evolutions, it is now possible to structure solutions, inconceivable until recently, in which companies have the potential to make intelligent use of large masses of unstructured data.

As an example of processing these large volumes of data, we have cases in which there are already companies processing petabytes of data, equivalent to 35 million files full of folders with text files or many years of HDTV content, with exceptional performance, to identify patterns of consumer behavior or find anomalies in e-commerce processes.

The adoption of Big Data does not only imply changes in companies, but also in academic and scientific segments, in research institutes and government companies.

It is important to highlight that we are still in the early stages of processing large volumes of data as a basis for planning and anticipating changes in the market and customer behavior.

From everything that has been exposed so far, you must have already concluded that Big Data is not just a tool, nor is it only a consequence of the evolution of database managers, but rather a convergence of several factors, technologies, consumers, computers in the context of the Internet.

And then we come to the concept of **Big Data** that we will adopt in this book:

A set of technologies to manage a huge volume of structured and unstructured data, at high speed, producing expected results in the expected timeframe to enable real-time analysis and planning.

There are those who think that Big Data is just another novelty, but when we talk about Big Data we are talking about technological innovations, new computational theories and new database managers.

The Big Data approach incorporates many different approaches to analytics to address a specific problem. Some analytics will be based on a traditional DW, while others utilize advanced predictive analytics.

Managing Big Data in a comprehensive, multidisciplinary and holistic way requires many different approaches to be successful in the company's business and in the planning of future strategies.

After performing indexing, structuring and cleaning processes of huge amounts of data, an interesting alternative to facilitate the analysis of these is to organize subsets, according to identified patterns or certain parameters, and make them accessible to the company's professionals.

One way to implement this data accessibility is to implement structured Data Warehouses in the company's business-oriented data marts. This approach offers compression, multi-level partitioning, and a great deal of processing parallelism.

"Successful implementation of Big Data requires not only investment in technology, but also in talented people and solid processes that allow you to extract valuable insights from data."

Doug Laney[8]

---

[8] He is a recognized professional in the field of data management and is best known for his contribution to the definition of the famous "3Vs" of Big Data: speed, variety and volume. He is the author of the article "3D Data Management: Controlling Data Volume, Velocity and Variety", published in 2001.

2 IMPLEMENTATION OF BIG DATA.

Achieving the greatest business value with Big Data requires not only investment in technology, but also the effective integration of that technology into the company's business processes. We cannot simply expect decision-makers to project future scenarios without fully understanding the results of the analyses and their operational context.

As pointed out by Stubbs (2014), it is essential for organizations to consider integrating Big Data into existing processes in order to maximize benefits and gain valuable insights. Here are some tips for a successful Big Data implementation, taking into account the need for integration with business processes:

1. Assess strategic objectives: Before beginning the implementation of Big Data, it is important to clearly understand the strategic objectives of the company. Identify key areas where the use of big data can have the greatest impact and align those goals with existing business processes.

2. Integration with business teams: Involving business teams from the beginning is key. Work collaboratively with the departments involved, such as marketing, sales, finance, operations, HR, and more, to understand their needs and how Big Data can add value to your processes.

3. Restructuring processes: Identify the changes needed in existing processes to properly incorporate Big Data. Assess whether there is a need for new workflows, adjustments to decision-making steps, or revision of operational strategies. Big Data should be used to optimize processes and improve efficiency.

4. Data management and governance: Establish a solid data management and governance framework. Define clear responsibilities for the collection, storage, security, and use of data, ensuring compliance with applicable regulations such as privacy and data protection.

5. Capacity building and training: Ensure that the team is properly qualified to deal with Big Data. Promote training and workshops so that employees understand how to use the available data analysis and interpretation tools. This will help integrate Big Data effectively into business processes, ensuring that everyone can extract maximum insights from the data collected.

6. Continuous tracking and monitoring: Big Data implementation should not be treated as an isolated project, but rather as an ongoing process. Establish metrics and performance indicators to measure the impact of Big Data on business processes. Conduct frequent follow-ups to assess the effectiveness of the analyses and make adjustments as needed.

7. Data culture: Foster an internal culture that values and actively uses data as a basis for decision-making. Encourage collaboration between teams by encouraging the sharing of information and insights gained through Big Data. This will help integrate the results of the analyses into the business processes more comprehensively and efficiently.

A very important factor in this context is the ability to integrate internal and external data sources composed of data from relational sources and the new forms of unstructured data.

2.1   Integration analysis.

Integration analysis must go through several steps, but there are essentially three steps to follow to structure the integration process: exploration, coding, and integration and incorporation.

They are explained below.

1º. Stage - Exploration.

In the early stages of analysis, it's natural to look for patterns in the data. Only by examining very large volumes of data, terabytes and petabytes, can the relationships and correlations between elements become apparent.

These patterns can provide information about the customer and preferences for a new product. You'll need to use a platform like Hadoop to organize your company's Big Data to look for these patterns.

As previously described, Hadoop is widely used as a building block for capturing and processing Big Data. Hadoop is designed with capabilities that speed up the processing of big data and make it capable of identifying patterns in large amounts of data in a relatively short period.

2º. Coding stage.

To make the leap from identifying a pattern to incorporating that trend into your business process, you need some sort of process to follow.

For example, if a large retailer monitors the media and identifies lots of talk about a football match or other event with high attendance near one of its stores, it will be able to plan what to do to promote the company at the event.

With hundreds of stores and many thousands of customers, it is necessary to establish a protocol for reacting to this type of information with processes that ensure effective marketing actions.

With a process in place, in the case of the sporting event example, the retailer can quickly take action and stock the nearby store with clothing and accessories bearing the logo of the teams participating in the event.

Once you've found something interesting in Big Data analytics, you need to structure it and make it a part of the company's business process.

It is necessary to make the connection between the analysis of your large structured and unstructured databases and your inventories of products and systems. To do this, it is necessary to integrate the data.

3º. Integration and incorporation stage.

Big Data is having a major impact on many aspects of data management.

Traditionally, integration data has focused on the movement of data through middleware, including message specifications and requirements for APIs.

These data integration concepts are more appropriate for managing data at rest than data in motion. The shift to the new world of unstructured data and streaming data changes the conventional notion of data integration.

If it is desirable to incorporate streaming data into your analysis to add another level of samples to your company's business process, it will be necessary to incorporate advanced technology so that everything is fast enough to allow decision-making in the necessary time.

Once the big data analysis is complete, you need to adopt an approach that allows you to integrate or incorporate the results of the analysis into your real-time business process of negotiations.

Businesses have high expectations of realizing real business value from big data analytics. In fact, many companies would like to begin a deep analysis of large volumes of internally generated data, such as log data security, which was not previously possible due to technological limitations.

Technologies for transporting large databases at high speed are requirements for integrating large distributed data sources.

Unstructured data sources often need to be moved quickly across large geographic distances for the sharing and collaboration needed on scientific research projects, for the development and delivery of content for the entertainment industry.

For example, scientific researchers typically work with very large data sets and now share data and collaborate more easily than in the past using a combination of big data analytics and the cloud.

To make good business decisions based on Big Data analysis, three basic principles apply:

Principle 1 – It is necessary to have a common understanding of data definitions.

- In the initial stage of using Big Data, it is common to seek to have a control similar to what was had over operational data.

- Once the most relevant standards for the company's business have been identified, it is necessary to map the given elements to a common definition.

- The definition is then applied to operational data, DW and other business databases.

Principle 2 – It is necessary to develop a set of services to qualify the data and make it consistent and reliable.

- When unstructured data and big data sources are integrated with structured operational data, you need to be sure that the results will be meaningful.

Principle 3 – You need a streamlined way to integrate your big data sources and operational data systems.

- Extract, transform, and load (ETL) technologies [9]have been used to accomplish this in data warehouse environments.

- The role of ETL is evolving to handle newer data management environments such as Hadoop.

In a big data environment, it may be necessary to combine tools that work in batch for integration processes, using ETL, with real-time integration and federation of data across multiple sources.

---

[9] Extract, transform and Load – ETL. Extraction, transformation and loading.

Data warehouses provide business users with a way to consolidate information across disparate sources such as enterprise resource planning and [10] customer relationship management to [11] analyze and report on data relevant to their specific business focus.

ETL tools, as shown in Figure 68, are used to transform the data into the format required by the Data Warehouse. The transformation is done in an intermediate area before the data is actually loaded into the Data Warehouse. Traditionally, ETL has been used with batch processing in data warehouse environments.

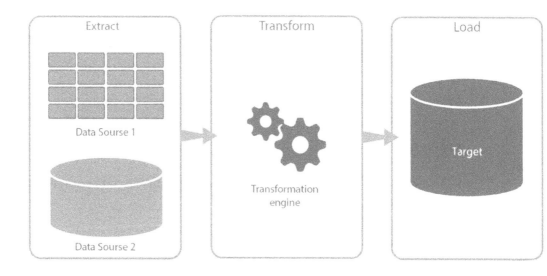

Figure 8 – ETL functions.

Many software vendors, including IBM, Informatica, Pervasive, Talend, and

---

[10] Enterprise Resource Planning - ERP. Enterprise Resource Planning refers to a set of software that companies use to manage day-to-day business activities, such as accounting, procurement, project management, risk and compliance management, and supply chain operations.

[11] Customer Relationship Management – CRM. The Customer Relationship Management system is used to record and organize all the points of contact that a consumer has with a company's salesperson.

Pentaho, provide ETL software tools.

ETL provides the infrastructure for integration, performing three important functions:

- Extraction. Read data from the database source.

- Transformation. Convert the extracted data so that it conforms to the requirements of the target database. The transformation is done using rules or merging data with other data.

- Load. Write data to the target database.

ETL is evolving to support integration beyond the data warehouse universe by supporting integration between transactional systems, data warehouses, BI platforms, MDM hubs, [12]cloud, and Hadoop platforms.

ETL software vendors are extending their solutions to provide big data extraction, transformation, and loading between Hadoop and traditional data management platforms.

ETL and software tools for other data integration processes, such as data cleansing, profiling, and auditing, work on different aspects of the data to ensure that it is considered trustworthy.

Data transformation is an essential process in the field of data management. It involves modifying the format, structure, or representation of data to make it compatible and usable by different applications, systems, or processes.

During data transformation, various operations can occur, such as converting data

---

[12] Mobile Device Management - MDM. Mobile Device Manager is a software that allows you to manage mobile devices such as smartphones, tablets, and laptops. In theory, its goal is to protect, monitor, manage, and support mobile devices, optimizing their functionality, the security of the communication network, and minimizing cost and downtime.

types, formatting dates, filtering and selecting specific columns, aggregating values, and so on. The main goal is to ensure that the data is adapted according to the needs and requirements of the applications or systems that will use it.

In addition, data transformation also involves cleaning and enriching data. This includes detecting and correcting errors, removing duplications, standardizing and normalizing data, and incorporating additional information from external sources to amplify the context and quality of the data.

Data transformation plays a crucial role in several areas, such as database management, data analysis, system migration, data integration, business intelligence, and many others. It is a fundamental process to ensure the interoperability and relevance of data, aiming at efficient and effective use in different applications and contexts. Data transformation tools aren't designed to work well with unstructured data. As a result, companies need to incorporate a significant amount of manual coding into their business process decision-making.

Considering the growth and importance of unstructured data for decision-making, ETL solutions from leading vendors are beginning to offer standardized approaches to transform unstructured data so that it can be more easily integrated with structured operational data.

Some big data sources, such as data from RFID tags[13] or sensors, have more well-established rules than social media data. The sensor data should be reasonably clean, although it is expected that some errors will be found.

---

[13] Radio Frequency IDentification - RFID. Radio Frequency Identification is a method of automatic identification through radio signals, retrieving and storing data remotely through devices called RFID tags. An RFID tag is a transponder, a small object that can be placed on a person, animal, equipment, packaging or product, among others.

2.2   Quality assurance.

Data quality assurance involves adopting a two-step process:

1. Look for standards in Big Data without having to worry about quality.

2. Once you've found your standards and established outcomes that are important to the business, apply the same data quality standards that apply to traditional data sources.

You want to avoid collecting and managing data that is not important to your business and that can corrupt other data elements in Hadoop or other big data platforms.

As you begin to incorporate the results of your big data analytics into your business process, recognize that high-quality data is essential for a company to make sound business decisions.

This is true for both big data and traditional data. Data quality refers to characteristics such as consistency, accuracy, reliability, completeness, timeliness, reasonableness, and validity.

Data quality software ensures that data elements are represented in the same way across different data stores or systems to increase data consistency.

For example, one data store might use two rows for a client's address, and another data store might use one row. This difference can result in inaccurate information about customers, such as one customer being identified as two different customers.

A corporation may use dozens of company name variations when it buys products. Data quality software can be used to identify all variations of the company name in your different databases and ensure that all information about your company's customers is consolidated.

This process is called providing a single view of the customer or product. Data quality software compares the data across different systems and cleans it up by removing redundancies.

2.3   Dealing with real-time data streams and complex event processing.

We begin this chapter with two questions:

- – What is data integration analytics?

- – How does this interfere with the transmission of large masses of data?

These are not simple questions to answer because there is a continuum of data management. Streaming computing is designed to handle a continuous stream of a large amount of unstructured data.

In contrast, complex event processing, CEP, [14]typically deals with a few variables that need to be correlated to a specific business process. In many situations, CEP is dependent on [15] data streams. However, zip code is not required for data streaming.

Like data flow, CEP relies on analyzing data streams in motion. In fact, if the data is at rest, it doesn't fall under the category of streaming data or zip code.

Data streaming is an analytical computing platform that stands out for its ability to process and analyze a continuous stream of data in real-time. Its main feature is that it deals with high-speed, usually unstructured, data from a variety of sources.

Unlike traditional data processing approaches, where data is first stored for further

---

[14] Complex Event Processing - CEP. Complex Event Processing has the problem of continuously matching incoming events to a pattern. The results of a match are usually complex events derived from the input events. In contrast to traditional DBMS, where a query is executed on stored data, CEP executes the data on a stored query.

[15] Streaming data is data that is continuously generated by thousands of data sources, which often send the data records simultaneously, in small sizes, on the order of kilobytes.

processing, data streaming allows you to analyze data as it arrives, in real-time. This approach has become essential in many applications that require quick decision-making and detection of patterns and insights in real time.

Data streaming applications are used in a variety of industries and scenarios, such as fraud detection in financial transactions, monitoring networks and systems, analyzing sensor data in IoT (Internet of Things) environments, real-time personalization on e-commerce platforms, analyzing social media data, among others.

Speed is one of the key aspects of data streaming, since these applications need to handle the agile and continuous processing of data in real-time. This involves implementing technologies and techniques that allow for the fast and efficient processing of this data, such as messaging systems, distributed processing, and streaming algorithms.

It should be noted that data streaming can also involve actions such as filtering, transforming, and enriching the data as it is ingested, to make it more relevant and useful for real-time analysis or actions.

This analytics platform has proven to be essential for generating immediate insights and agile decision-making in various business contexts. Therefore, the data is continuously analyzed and transformed into memory before being stored on a disk.

Processing data streams works by processing data in "time windows" in memory on a *cluster* of servers.

This is similar to the data-at-rest management approach leveraging Hadoop. The main difference is speed. In the Hadoop cluster, data is collected in *batch* mode and then processed.

Speed matters less in Hadoop than in *continuous data* streaming.

A few key principles define the situation in which using *streams* is the most appropriate:

1. When it is necessary to determine a retail sales opportunity at the time of choice, either through social media or through message-based permission.

2. Collecting information about the movement on a secure website.

3. To be able to react to an event that needs an immediate response, such as a service interruption or a change in a patient's medical condition.

4. Real-time calculation of costs that are dependent on variables.

According to Gualtieri (2013), data streaming is useful when analytics need to be done in real time, while the data is in motion. In fact, the value of analytics decreases over time. For example, if your business can't analyze and act immediately, a sales opportunity may be missed or a threat may go undetected.

An important factor regarding streaming data is the fact that it is a *single-pass*[16] analysis, i.e., the analyst cannot reanalyze the data after it is transmitted. This is common in applications where one is looking for the absence of data.

Most data management professionals are familiar with the need to manage metadata in structured database management environments.

These data sources are designed to operate with metadata and are strongly typed, an example is when we have, in an attribute, a string in which the first ten characters correspond to the first name of a customer.

It is possible to assume that metadata is non-existent in unstructured data, but this is not true. You can usually find metadata in any type of data.

From this metadata implicit in unstructured data, you can analyze the information

---

[16] Single-Pass is a compiler that passes source code through each compilation unit only once.

using XML[17]. XML is a technique for presenting unstructured text files with meaningful tags. This technology is not new and was a foundational technology for the implementation of service orientation.

Examples of products for streaming data include IBM InfoSphere Streams, Twitter's Storm, and Yahoo S4.

So, what's the difference between CEP and data streaming solutions? While streaming computing is typically applied to analyze large amounts of data in real-time, CEP is much more focused on solving a specific use case based on events and actions.

Both data streaming and CEP have a huge impact on how businesses can make strategic use of Big Data.

With streaming data, businesses can process and analyze this data in real-time to gain immediate insight.

With CEP, companies can stream data and leverage a business process engine to apply business rules to the results of data streaming analysis.

---

[17] eXtensible Markup Language – XML. It is a markup language recommended by the W3C for creating documents with hierarchically organized data, such as texts, databases, or vector drawings.

"Dealing with the costs associated with Big Data can be a significant challenge for organizations. It is critical to establish a clear cost management strategy from the outset and adopt flexible approaches to optimize the balance between the benefits and the investments required."

Dan Vesset[18]

[18] Leader of IDC's global research operations, ensuring the availability of effective and efficient processes and tools to IDC's global analyst community.

3   SPEAKING OF COSTS.

After collection and analysis, Big Data will provide avenues to solve existing challenges and also subsidize solutions to problems that have not yet been identified. Despite companies being aware of the potential of Big Data to solve previously unsolvable problems, the process comes at a high cost.

Figure 9 – Value versus Price.

Operational processes, as discussed earlier, will need to be changed to accommodate Big Data. New data types will need to be added to the environment. In addition, new types of analytics will emerge to help understand the implications of Big Data and how it relates, or does not, to existing data (Widjaya, 2019)

To understand the financial impact of costs and investments to have Big Data in the company, it is necessary to examine the constraints for it to produce results. This exam should consider:

- The identification of the data sources that will be handled by Big Data.

- The impact on the company's processes by modifications to already established business processes or by the creation of new processes.

- The changes in technology or new technologies that will be necessary for the incorporation of Big Data in the company's technology park.

- The search for and acquisition of new talent and upgrades to existing talent.

- The ROI potential of Big Data investments.

It is also necessary to examine these constraints from two perspectives and try to understand the relationship between the economic impacts and the advantages of Big Data:

- The costs to deploy Big Data.

- The costs to keep Big Data operational.

3.1   The initial cost: infrastructure.

When we approach Big Data infrastructure, we are referring to a wide range of physical components and resources required to support and operate the complex Big Data platforms. This infrastructure includes a number of interconnected technologies, which work together to collect, store, process, and transmit large volumes of data.

First and foremost, the company needs to rely on specialized tools to collect the data. This could involve implementing sensors, monitoring devices, or even extraction and tracking software. These tools are responsible for capturing raw data from different sources, such as internal company systems, mobile devices, social networks, IoT (Internet of Things) sensors, and many others.

Once the data is collected, a proper storage system is required to ensure that it is kept secure and accessible. Generally, this entails utilizing a database management system (DBMS) or even a data warehouse, which allows for efficient storage and organization of data. The choice of storage system depends on the specific needs of the business, such as the volume of data, the frequency of access, and the complexity of queries.

In addition, it is essential to have a powerful software system to process the data. This can include the use of specific frameworks and programming languages for Big Data, such as Hadoop, Spark, or Apache Cassandra, which offer advanced capabilities for large-scale data processing and analysis.

These tools allow for the execution of sophisticated algorithms, the application of machine learning models, and the performance of complex analyses, which help to extract valuable insights from the data.

An efficient computer network is necessary to transmit the data quickly and reliably. This involves utilizing high-speed networking technologies, proper routers and switches, and secure communication protocols.

It is important that all elements of the Big Data infrastructure are interconnected in an efficient manner to ensure smooth and uninterrupted data transmission.

In addition to these essential components, Big Data infrastructure can also involve other elements such as high-performance servers, cloud storage systems, security systems to protect data from cyber threats, virtualization and scalability techniques to handle the continuous growth of data, among others. Every business can adapt and scale its infrastructure according to its specific needs.

Importantly, Big Data infrastructure requires significant investments in terms of financial, technological, and expertise resources. Businesses need to have a skilled team to design, implement, and manage this complex infrastructure. Additionally, it is essential to keep up with trends and technological advancements in this area, as the field of Big Data is constantly evolving.

However, the biggest expense that businesses incur when dealing with Big Data is the cost of the analytics database. The cost of big data platforms, such as Hadoop and Spark, will scale proportionally to the amount of storage, compute, and processing power the company uses.

Most of the time, the platform needs additional tools to actually perform Big Data analytic operations. An essential piece of software is Hadoop. A Hadoop cluster can be managed from anywhere, from a single node to a potentially undefined number. The recommended minimum number of nodes is three, since Hadoop achieves fault tolerance by duplicating files on each of these nodes.

It is recommended that each of these clusters be at least a mid-range Intel server, which costs[19] between $4,000 and $6,000 for 3TB and 6TB of disk space. A good rule of thumb is to assume it will cost $1,000 - $2,000 per TB. A 1 petabyte Hadoop cluster will cost around $1 million since it needs around 200 nodes.

3.2   The cost of management and maintenance.

The initial cost of purchasing a big data management system is only a fraction of the total investment required to implement and maintain an efficient big data infrastructure. While purchasing or licensing a specific piece of software may require an upfront outlay, the ongoing costs associated with managing and maintaining that system are critical to ensuring its proper functioning and making the most of its potential.

Managing a Big Data system involves a number of fundamental activities, such as the continuous integration of new data sources, the cleaning and transformation of data, the configuration and adjustment of processing and analysis processes, and the constant monitoring of the infrastructure to ensure its performance and stability.

In addition, maintaining a Big Data system requires continuous attention to security updates and fixes, performance and capacity enhancements, as well as keeping up with the development of new technologies and methodologies in the field of Big Data. This often requires a specialized team dedicated to system administration and technical support.

The complexity and scale of big data systems can also bring additional costs, such as

---

[19] Values calculated in September 2019.

the need for large-scale data storage resources, high-performance servers, robust network infrastructure, and advanced security measures. These costs can include investments in hardware, additional software, software licenses, cloud services, and even hiring external experts.

It is also important to consider that the analysis and use of Big Data data requires specialized skills and knowledge, which may involve qualification and training for the internal team, or even the hiring of consultants and specialized professionals.

In this way, the total cost of Big Data goes far beyond the initial investment in the management system. It covers recurring management and maintenance costs, as well as ongoing investments in hardware, software, security, training, and technical support.

It is also important to factor in overhead costs, such as the time and resources required to implement and integrate the big data system into the company's existing operations.

It is essential to understand that managing and maintaining a Big Data system requires an ongoing commitment to ensuring data quality and reliability. This involves adopting data governance practices, implementing cybersecurity policies, constantly monitoring data integrity, and ensuring compliance with applicable regulations and standards.

Another key aspect is the constant evolution of the Big Data system. As the demands and needs of the business change, it is necessary to adapt the system to ensure that it continues to meet objectives and expectations. This may involve expanding storage capacity, improving data processing performance, incorporating new technologies and advanced analytics techniques, among others.

Importantly, the total cost of Big Data can vary significantly depending on the size and complexity of the company, the amount of data to be processed, the technological resources required, and other factors. Therefore, it is necessary to make a careful analysis of the costs involved and carry out strategic planning to maximize the return on investment.

The additional costs start accumulating to the original amount as soon as the company feels the need to adjust the sizing of its operations. What was once a 6 TB cluster may need to scale up to more than 200 petabytes of storage space, handling hundreds of thousands of nodes.

> *This presents an even bigger problem than simply paying for the cost of additional storage space and processing power.*

More infrastructure means more people are needed to manage it, which brings us to the more variable cost implication of adopting a big data platform.

3.3   The cost of human capital.

The technology segment is one of the fastest evolving sectors there is. As a direct result, data science has quickly exploded into one of the most popular career options for new university graduates.

However, being a relatively new field means that there aren't as many professionals to make it as accessible as in other industries.

A full-time Hadoop specialist will cost between $90,000 and $180,000 per year, while outsourced work costs an average of $81-$100 per hour. The cost of development varies greatly depending on the developer's experience, their location, and the size of the project.

Business analysts will need to consider increasing their ranks with data scientists. This can be accomplished with the support of consultancies in the start-up phases, but should evolve into a permanent team as the direction and benefits become clearer.

Hiring a single data scientist doesn't seem like a good answer. Unless your company is medium-sized and doesn't have many products and situations to analyze.

Better results will be obtained by creating a team of data scientists tasked with discovering Big Data sources, analyzing analytical processes, and managing impacts on business processes (Davenport, 2014) (Davenport et al., 2012).

For the IT team, knowledge of new Big Data technologies will need to be introduced to existing teams through training and mentoring. Consulting resources can and should be employed to help your company get started with its big data initiatives.

Data scientists are responsible for modeling complex business problems, uncovering business insights, and identifying opportunities.

They bring to work:

• Ability to integrate and prepare large and varied datasets

• Advanced analysis and modeling skills to reveal and understand shaky relationships

• Business knowledge to apply context

• Communication skills to deliver results

Data science is an emerging field. Demand is high, and finding qualified personnel is one of the main challenges associated with big data analytics. A data scientist may be based in IT or in the business – but wherever he or she is, he or she will be your new best friend and collaborator in the planning and implementation of big data analytics projects (Davenport et al., 2012).

Data science is an interdisciplinary field, made up of computer science, mathematics, and statistics, and the specialization of the domain in which the data derives.

The following figure shows the intersection between the three fields.

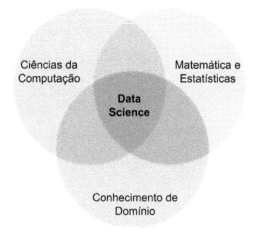

Figure 69—Data Science

The goal of data science is to harness the power of data to gain valuable insights and turn them into knowledge that underpins rational decision-making. Achieving this goal requires a diverse set of skills and knowledge, which span areas such as mathematics, statistics, programming, and mastery of the field of study in which the data is being analyzed.

A data scientist is a highly valued and sought-after professional in today's market due to their ability to extract meaningful insights from data. This professional needs to have solid knowledge in mathematics and statistics to understand the statistical methods and techniques applicable to data analysis. In addition, mastery of programming is essential for dealing with large volumes of data and applying machine learning algorithms and statistical modeling techniques.

However, finding a professional with this skill set and expertise can be challenging, as the demand for data scientists significantly outstrips the supply of skilled professionals. This scarcity creates a rarity in today's market.

Not only do data scientists possess advanced technical knowledge, but they also need to have an analytical mind and be able to formulate appropriate questions to guide their analysis. They must have the communication skills to translate the complex results into understandable insights for decision-makers. The ability to lead projects and work in a team is also important, as data science often involves collaboration with experts in different fields.

The market is increasingly aware of the importance of data science and is investing in the training and development of these rare professionals. Universities, online courses, and training programs are popping up to meet the demand for data science experts.

The skills required by a data scientist can be divided into seven categories:

1. Programming. The main programming languages used are Python and R. Another highly sought-after computer knowledge is SQL.

2. Work with data. It boils down to collecting, cleaning, and transforming the data to be utilized.

3. Descriptive statistics. Application of various techniques to describe and summarize a dataset.

4. Data visualization. Knowledge and use of tools to transform data into interpretable graphs.

5. Statistical model. Creation of statistical models and use of them for statistical inference and hypothesis testing.

6. Dealing with Big Data. Using tools required due to the large volumes of data processed.

7. Machine learning. Knowledge and creation of Machine Learning algorithms for decision making and prediction.

The main tools that a data scientist uses are presented in the following figure.

In almost every poll, these two are often tied in terms of popularity. However, both languages have their strengths and weaknesses.

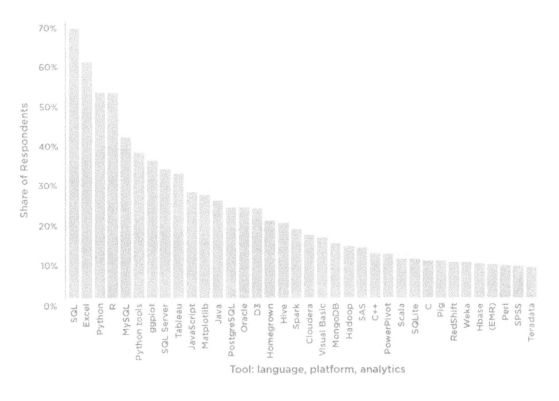

Figure 10 — Most used Data Science tools.

On the X-axis, we have the name of the tool, which includes programming languages, data platforms, or analysis tools. On the Y-axis, we have the percentage of respondents who report that they use the corresponding tool.

As we can see, the most used tool is SQL. The next tool is Excel, a simple yet very powerful tool. After that, there are two tied programming languages: Python and R. These two languages are the darlings of the Data Science world.

And what does the data scientist's job look like? We can summarize this work in 6 activities presented in the following figure.

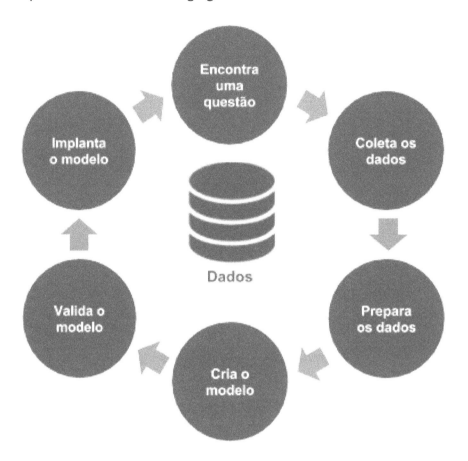

Figure 11 — The work of the data scientist.

Here's how the Data Science process works:

1st. One question, yet to be answered, needs to be found. It could be a hypothesis that needs to be tested, a decision that needs to be made, or something you want to try to predict.

2nd. Data is collected for analysis. Sometimes this means designing an experiment to create new data, other times the data already exists and you need to find it.

3rd.   The collected data is prepared for analysis. It's a process often referred to as data munging or data wrangling. In this process, the data is cleaned and transformed into a format suitable for analysis.

4th.   A model is created for the data. In the most generic sense, this can be a numerical model, a visual model, a statistical model, or a machine learning model. Once created, the model is used to provide evidence for or against a hypothesis, to help make a decision or predict an outcome.

5th.   The model is validated. It is determined whether the model answers the question, helps with decision-making, or returns an accurate prediction. In addition, it is necessary to ratify whether the model created is the appropriate one, taking into account the data and context.

6th.   The model is deployed. This may mean communicating the results of the analysis to others, making a decision, and taking action or putting an application into production.

Data science can be thought of as an ongoing process. The cycle described above repeats several times, and with each iteration, learnings and improvements are deployed to the model. It is interesting to note that the process is often not sequential, it is often necessary to skip steps backwards or forwards as problems arise and learnings about better solutions are discovered.

3.4   The costs of Data Security and Governance.

Data Security and Governance play a key role in the Big Data landscape, where the amount, variety, and speed of data generated and processed are ever-increasing. Protecting data from cyber threats, complying with data protection regulations, and enforcing appropriate governance practices are essential to ensure data integrity, confidentiality, and availability.

When it comes to implementing cybersecurity measures in the context of Big Data, it's crucial to take a comprehensive approach and layers of defense-in-depth. This involves the use of firewalls, data encryption, intrusion detection systems, access control, and authentication, among other security measures. Additionally, implementing data security practices at every stage of the data collection, storage, processing, and sharing process is critical to protecting sensitive information from theft, leakage, or unauthorized breaches.

Regarding compliance with data protection regulations, companies must ensure that they are compliant with applicable laws and regulations, such as the GDPR in the European Union or the LGPD in Brazil. This involves appointing a data protection officer, conducting data protection impact assessments, implementing appropriate technical and organisational security measures, as well as ensuring the rights of data subjects, such as the right to privacy and to be forgotten.

Data governance in the context of Big Data is another crucial aspect of ensuring the proper and effective use of data. Setting clear data management policies, standardizing metadata, creating data catalogs, monitoring performance and data quality, are all practices that contribute to robust data governance. In addition, implementing data governance processes enables organizations to maximize the value of data, reduce exposure risks, and ensure compliance with current regulations.

A practical example of effective implementation of data security and governance in the context of Big Data can be observed in a financial institution. In this highly regulated and sensitive landscape, the use of advanced cybersecurity technologies, such as next-generation firewalls, encryption of data at rest and in transit, and continuous threat monitoring, is essential to protect the confidentiality and integrity of customers' financial information.

Additionally, implementing a robust data governance program that includes setting clear data management policies, creating consistent metadata, and establishing a data governance committee, helps ensure that data is managed ethically, securely, and in compliance with financial industry laws and regulations.

3.5   Miscellaneous custodians of big data.

The factors presented so far provide a good representation of how much Big Data costs, but the issue doesn't stop there, most of the time. The cost of the factors that fall under this section depend mainly on the particularities of the company.

Among them, the following can be mentioned.

3.5.1 Legacy technology and migration costs.

The rapid evolution of technology has led many companies to face challenges related to legacy technology and migration costs. A notable example of this situation concerns Hadoop, a platform for processing big data that many experts consider to be becoming obsolete. However, for companies that already have Hadoop integrated into their data pipelines, migrating to new solutions can be a complex and costly task.

Reliance on legacy technology puts companies in a position of vulnerability, as business demands and requirements are always evolving. The adoption of new software solutions becomes essential to meet new challenges and remain competitive in the market.

The costs involved in migrating from legacy technology to more modern solutions are another significant challenge. In addition to the high financial investments required, the migration may also require a great effort to train and reskill internal teams. This can impact the company's operational efficiency during the transition process.

However, it is crucial for businesses to consider the long-term benefits of migrating to new technology solutions. By adopting more up-to-date technologies, organizations can gain competitive advantages such as improvements in agility, scalability, and performance. In addition, upgrading the technological infrastructure can enable the adoption of new business strategies, allowing the incorporation of advanced data analytics, artificial intelligence, and machine learning.

3.5.2 Network costs.

The average company often underestimates the impact of network costs on their operations. While the cost of transferring data over the Internet may seem low and negligible for small amounts of data, this changes dramatically when dealing with large volumes of information.

For businesses dealing with terabytes or even petabytes of data, bandwidth costs can quickly become significant. As the demand for data transfer increases, whether through uploads, downloads, streaming, or any other form of online communication, network spending begins to pile up.

These costs can come from different sources, such as internet providers or cloud services used for data storage and transfer. Depending on the specifics of the contract and the needs of the business, bandwidth can become a major expense to consider in the budget.

Also, it's worth noting that network costs aren't just limited to data transfer. You also need to factor in the costs related to maintaining, upgrading, and expanding the company's network infrastructure. This entails investments in equipment, servers, routers, firewalls, and other components necessary to ensure a reliable and secure network.

Given this, it is essential for companies to do an in-depth analysis of their network costs and adopt efficient strategies to optimize these expenses. This may involve implementing more efficient data management policies, such as compression and deduplication, using caching technologies, monitoring network traffic to identify bottlenecks and inefficiencies, and more.

3.5.3   Proxy providers.

When it comes to collecting data from the web as part of a big data strategy, it's important to consider the cost of proxy providers. Proxy providers play an essential role, allowing businesses to collect large amounts of data efficiently and without overloading the target servers. However, these services often come at an associated cost, especially as the amount of data collected increases.

When using web scraping, the process of automated data collection, it is common for businesses to make multiple requests over time. Each request involves an interaction with the proxy provider, which redirects the request to the desired web server and returns the collected data. Depending on the volume of requests and the size of the data collected, the proxy provider's monthly bill can increase significantly.

Given this scenario, it is important for businesses to make a careful selection of the proxy provider, taking into account their needs and budget. There are several tools available in the market that help you compare the features and prices offered by the various providers. These tools can take into account factors such as the number of requests allowed, connection speed, quality of technical support, and scalability options.

By choosing the proper proxy provider, businesses can ensure efficient utilization of resources and avoid any unpleasant surprises on monthly bills. Additionally, it is critical to conduct a periodic analysis of the costs involved in using proxy providers, as data needs and volumes can change over time.

3.5.4   Data preservation costs.

When it comes to preserving data, we often don't realize the cost involved in this process. Taking regular snapshots of data is essential to ensure the security and integrity of the information stored, but this also entails additional costs.

One of the most common options for data preservation is to create regular backups, which can be done on both physical devices and cloud storage services. However, these backups incur costs, both in terms of the additional storage required and in relation to the computational resources used during the process of creating the backups.

Additionally, depending on the amount of data and how often backups are created, costs can increase significantly. This is especially true for companies that deal with large volumes of data or that need to comply with specific regulations regarding data preservation.

Another important factor to consider is the costs of recovering the data in the event of a loss or failure. If an incident occurs and data needs to be restored from backups, additional resources are required to perform that recovery. This may involve specialized services, such as hiring data recovery consultants, or allocating in-house time and resources to deal with the issue.

In order to properly account for data preservation costs, it is essential to take into account all related aspects, such as the additional storage required, the computational resources used to create backups, and the possibility of additional costs in the event of data recovery.

Companies should conduct a careful analysis of their data preservation requirements and determine the best strategy that meets their needs while also being economically viable. This can involve adopting more efficient storage and backup technologies, properly allocating resources, and creating data preservation policies that balance security with costs.

"The goal is to turn data into information and information into insights."

Carly Fiorina[20]

---

[20] Carly Fiorina began her career in the 1980s at the telecommunications company AT&T, where she rose to executive positions. He rose to the top as CEO (1999-2005) and Chairman of the Board (2000-2005) of Hewlett-Packard, a technology company. She has come to be considered one of the most powerful women in the United States.

4   HIDDEN BIG DATA LURES

Unfortunately, the considerations about Big Data costs do not end with the items discussed in the previous section. If you interrupt your calculations without considering the items covered in this section, you will not have a comprehensive analysis of the true cost of data management operations.

The main sources of hidden costs are:

1   Inefficient data integration.

Deriving value from enterprise data typically requires it to be transformed and integrated. If the data integration solution adopted by the company involves a lot of manual effort, redundancy, or other types of inefficiencies, it can be a major source of hidden costs in the form of wasted staff time and unnecessary infrastructure.

2   Unnecessary backups.

File storage can be simple and inexpensive for the typical PC user – they have a few hundred GB of documents, photos, and videos on their hard drive. Things are much more expensive and complicated in a company. A company has a lot more files to deal with and needs to make sure those files are safe.

Backup, recovery, and archiving are the most important storage technology segment among organizations. Backups are even more popular than virtualization and cloud computing.

The company should always back up its data. However, if you're backing up your data more often than you need to, or storing more copies than you need, you may not be operating as cost-effectively as possible.

It is necessary to have assurance that the right level of data backups are being performed, but not more.

3   Low-quality data.

Data riddled with quality issues is likely to cost much more to store, integrate, and analyze than error-free data. While avoiding data quality issues entirely may not be possible, fixing data quality issues through automated tools can help you minimize the costs you incur due to poor data quality.

4   Uninformed employees

Are the data scientists on your team conscientious professionals? Or do they totally lack an understanding of data management best practices?

In the latter case, a lack of commitment and dedication can increase Big Data costs, creating data quality bottlenecks and errors whenever someone who isn't a professional data scientist touches the data.

Avoid this hidden cost of big data by turning your employees into collaborating data scientists.

4.1   Alleviating the large cost of Big Data.

A big data platform is too expensive to manage for the average business, but this cost can be greatly reduced in a number of ways. The most important of these is to leverage managed and open-source Big Data platforms.

One of the consequences of the popularity of cloud-based software is the proliferation of proprietary, managed, and open-source software. This is opposed to licensed and on-premise solutions, respectively.

As big data matures, it will be necessary to consider new evolving data types and new data sources. Some of them can be controlled, while others will control some of what is done.

The most important decisions you need to make regarding types and fonts are:

- How often will you need to interact with the data?

- Can you trust the data sources and the data itself?

- What can be done with the data?

- What data will be needed to address your business problem?

- Who owns the data and the products of the work?

- How long is it necessary to preserve the data collected?

- Where can your business find the data sources it needs?

Let's exemplify this context. Let's assume that your company owns a brand of toothpaste and is part of a corporation in the personal care segment. It is very likely that it is a desire of the company to use Big Data technology to be able to understand the needs, buying habits and loyalty of customers.

From these requirements, it will be necessary to find data on customer sentiment and experience, while looking for data on how the customer views the competitive alternatives available in the market.

Some of this data will be available in traditional databases and systems, such as customer relationship management (CRM) systems and data warehouses.

But unfortunately, it's very likely that your company is looking to broaden its analytics base beyond traditional data sources and will need to understand where to source these new data sources.

Getting the data is, then, the first job to be done. Here it is not only a matter of knowing where to get the data, but also the form or type of the data as well as the quality and reliability of the data.

Good sources of sentiment data are found on social media, such as Facebook, Foursquare, Yelp, Pinterest, and Twitter. The fonts that will be selected can be determined by the habits of your customers.

For example, your ideal customer, the persona, may be very active on social media. However, your company can only operate in the business-to-business mode[21] of selling.

In this case, it is necessary to seriously analyze whether social media sites will contribute to the understanding of your customers more proactively. You'll need to find important B2B websites to incorporate into your big data analytics.

The problem is as big as the sheer amount of data and the data sought is a grain of sand on the beach. The few snippets of messages that are information about the customer's sentiment towards the product are hidden in the vastness of the Internet.

Additionally, the structure and types of this data vary from site to site, adding additional complexity and many costs. The company will need to understand the value of sifting through this data to get the supporting insights.

Some of these sources can be easily examined at a low cost, while others will require a more detailed ROI to determine the potential value of information about the company.

After identifying the sources and types of data, the company must then understand what can be done with the data. To do so, some questions about the data need to be asked:

- Can they be modified?

---

[21] Business to Business - B2B. It refers to the type of business done from company to company rather than directly with the consumer. B2B companies are those that provide services to other companies, usually as outsourced companies.

- Can they be stored locally for later use?

- Are there any limits on the amount of data that can be gathered in a given period?

- How often can data be obtained?

- How often does the data change at the source?

The answers to these questions can help the company understand the economic impacts of using Big Data and may raise new questions:

- What is the impact on analysis of not having unrestricted access to a particular source?

- How important is constant access?

- What will be the impact on revenue and product marketing decisions if a given data source is accessed only once a week?

The answers generate other questions until one has a satisfactory view of this scenario.

It is also necessary to understand how often data is used by internal systems can help control costs.

If it is included in the requirements that it is necessary to analyze customer sentiment in real time, the cost to analyze time-related attributes will cause a significant increase in costs.

The cost generated only when you need to use the data is significantly lower and is more manageable.

Another cost-saving factor is to consider whether the analysis may not be as fast or with less data source. Data usage and currency are key factors in analyzing the Big Data economy.

Some data source vendors for Big Data charge to release ownership of your data, license it for specific use, or release it for non-destructive use. Others are more flexible, charging little to no access costs or excessive usage requirements.

The company, in the example, will need to look at each source and ensure that proper care is taken regarding who owns the data and who owns the work products that use the data.

Figure 12 – It is necessary to monitor costs.

Some licensing data may limit usage for calculation and disposal. You can use the data as part of a process analysis, but you must then delete the data at the completion of the calculations.

Other vendors may allow you to use the data, but require you to purge this data when your analysis and calculations are complete, returning the calculations and analyses to increase the value of the data source to other customers.

Great care must be taken to protect company information and work products as you integrate Big Data into your work environment.

In the previous example, the company might want to include a certain period of time in the requirements that check customer sentiment. To meet this new requirement, new questions will be generated:

- Has the customer changed their sentiment towards the brand in the last month? Six months? A year?

- How did the customer behave in relation to the competition's offerings in the same periods?

Knowing how often the company needs to access data can help predict the costs associated with data capacity, accessibility, and currency.

Once you've decided on the approach that will best contribute to achieving your company's business objectives, you can begin to operationalize that approach. The ability to operationalize the approach chosen to leverage Big Data will allow your business to move to the steady state of the economy, the state where costs are known and stabilized and data sources have proven reliable and useful.

However, over time, costs may change due to rate and licensing corrections, and new issues may become important. However, your company will have the right foundation.

Continuing with the example, the company needs to understand how its processes will be affected. You need to decide whether to identify new customers and add them, as prospects, to customer databases.

In other cases, you'll need to create processes to understand how Big Data can be used to create understandings about your products or seek deeper understandings about customer loyalty and retention.

In any of these cases, it is important to model the costs needed to change existing work processes. The true economic impact of Big Data will require balancing the costs of such changes with the potential benefit.

The next step in deploying Big Data is to understand the impacts of the technology. It would be great if we could continue to use a lot of existing technologies and applications in the company when Big Data is applied in the workflow.

However, it is more likely that new technologies will be needed to extract the maximum economic value from Big Data investments. As discussed earlier, many new and different tools are available for Big Data.

Existing technologies are very fragile because they were designed for a specific task or because they are too simplistic to solve the stress of large data applications.

In the example, the needs of the company will create processes and technologies. Each of these requirements will drive the need for new skills and modernization of existing skills in many departments, but most visibly in the IT department and business analyst areas.

All of the costs discussed above should be balanced against the potential results of the investments. In the next phase, we need to look at the ROI for Big Data.

4.2   Making easy something difficult.

Now that you have a better understanding of what you need to do to introduce Big Data into your business, think about how you can accomplish it. Here are some tips to consider when bringing Big Data into your business:

Tip 1 – Hire those who already know.

- Don't object to hiring one or two experts as consultants.

- If they know the context of Big Data deployment well, they are able to mentor their teams.

Tip 2 – Hire good training.

- Take courses and read books on the subject.

- Do research on Big Data on the Internet.

- Participate in discussion groups.

- Attend industry conferences and events.

Dica 3 - Experiment.

- Plan for failure. Rapid failure is becoming mandatory for contemporary technology-driven companies. The best lessons learned often come from failures.

- Study other people's experiences.

Tip 4 – Set proper expectations.

- Correctly set expectations can mean the difference between success and failure.

- A successful project can be seen as a failure if the business benefits are exaggerated or if it takes 50% longer to deliver.

- Big Data offers enormous potential, but only if costs and time for its implementation are calculated correctly.

Tip 5 – Be holistic.

- Try to look at all dimensions for any big data data initiative.

- If the project is delivered on time and on budget, but the end users are not trained or ready to use it, the project may result in failure.

- The most successful project managers understand that good outcomes need to be thought of as a whole that includes people, processes, and technology.

"Big data is a journey, not a destination."

Michael Dell[22]

---

[22] Founder and CEO of Dell.

5   BIG DATA FOR SMALL BUSINESSES.

There is no doubt that Big Data is one of the major trends for the most diverse sectors of the market in the coming years. A survey by Gartner shows that, by 2030, three out of four companies intend to invest in Big Data in their business. But is it possible to develop Big Data solutions for small businesses as well?

Over time, since the concept of Big Data began to become better known, starting in 2008, an idea was created that this tool would only be possible to be applied in large companies. After all, they are able to afford costs, create departments focused on the topic, and structure ways to monitor large volumes of data.

But that's not true. Increasingly, small businesses are using Big Data to help solve issues that are important in their day-to-day lives. Every day, 2.5 quintillillion bytes of information are generated on the internet every day. And in that number everything fits — the post on the social network, the report of a bank transaction, a GIF sent by a messaging app, a heart *emoji*.

There are millions of possibilities and that doesn't mean you should look at all of them. It would be impossible and a huge waste of time (Kamioka et al., 2014).

However, several tools can be useful to analyze a large volume of information that is really useful for your business. To do this, the first step is to know exactly what you want with Big Data.

See this and other tips below.

1. Have a goal with Big Data.

    First and foremost, using Big Data for small businesses must start from a concrete goal. Where do you want to go with the analysis of a given volume of data? Answering this question is crucial for the development of your business from Big Data.

    If your goal is to invest in user experience, for example, it is important to filter the data that is generated on social networks, such as comments, photos, stories, reviews on sales sites, recommendations, among others.

From an analysis of the raw information collected in the most diverse channels, it is possible to identify the actions that should be implemented in order to increase engagement with these people.

If your focus, at this moment, is to build customer loyalty and ensure future sales from those who already know you, filter the information obtained by forms, sales data, comments on social networks to develop strategies for the future.

2. Know your customer's habits.

   Large supermarket or pharmacy companies know very well who their customers are and try, in any case, to standardize behaviors with the sole purpose of increasing sales.

   Don't be surprised if one day you walk into an establishment and find the diaper shelf next to the beer shelf on a Friday night.

   It's very unlikely that this is just a coincidence. In fact, it is the analysis of thousands of purchases over time through Big Data tools and cross-referencing several different types of data. It's like putting down a buying profile of your average customer on paper.

   In the case of a small business, logic can also be adopted. Big data for small businesses can help find consumption patterns that can convert into increased sales.

3. Keep an eye on the metrics.

   Another way to use Big Data for small businesses is to focus on metrics in the online environment.

   Cross-referencing sales data from e-commerce platforms with sponsored campaigns on Facebook, for example, can help define the best time for scheduling ads or the type of audience that has to receive these posts. The trick is to analyze the data and test.

4. Don't dismiss information.

    Although it is not recommended that a small business wants to "embrace the world" from Big Data, it is also recommended not to neglect information that is generated in sales and can be easily collected.

    It may be that, at first glance, you don't see anything wrong with knowing the neighborhood where your client lives. However, it is precisely this information that can make the difference when designing a campaign.

    Try to check for hidden trends within the data volumes. Deciphering these "stories" behind the raw reports can mean the leap you need to amplify your performance in a particular location or segment.

5. Shapeless always.

    The Big Data market is constantly changing. Every day we are faced with the discovery of new tools and ways of seeing and analyzing the data generated by various sources. It's important to stay up-to-date on industry news and keep an open mind to innovate whenever you need to.

    Several experts have treated information as the main strategic asset of companies in the 21st century. And they're not wrong. The important thing is to know what information is necessary and desirable, how to get to it, and how to analyze it. It's a good challenge.

5.1   3 Big Data Tools for Small Businesses.

Big Data tools can be used by virtually any business. The important thing is to know the available technology and be aware of the desired results.

Technology opens up possibilities for small and medium-sized business owners. Entrepreneurs can also benefit from technology to plan for the future of their company.

In the last ten years, small and medium-sized companies have gained a competitive advantage, as they now have access to information with the same agility as large companies, without the need for large investments.

Some of the solutions can, in fact, be free for the company. There are free, open-source public databases and cross-referencing systems that can be customized as needed.

The special labor and necessary infrastructure, however, do not come cheap. Therefore, it may not pay for a small business to hire a specialized professional, but it is always possible to hire a consultancy.

Here are 3 recommended tools at low or no cost that can be used by small and medium-sized businesses:

1. Google Analytics

    Google's free tool has interesting solutions with features that can be used by small businesses.

Figure 13 – Google Analytics.

The main purpose of Google Analytics is not only to know how many users access a website, but also how these users behave when navigating through the various pages and sections of this website.

It is based on the information collected that it is possible to analyze whether visitors have the expected behavior as a response to a certain online marketing campaign.

Traffic monitoring is one of the main functions of any online activity and indispensable for business management in this segment, and Google Analytics, or GA as it is also known, is the standard tool on the market.

2. ClearStory Data

ClearStory Data is a scalable, cloud-based business intelligence solution that enables enterprises, organizations, and departments to uncover business insights and collaborate on them.

ClearStory

DATA

New You See It

Figure 14 – ClearStory Data.

The solution combines data from disparate sources and generates actionable, interactive insights that users can tap into. It is used in various industries that include manufacturing, retail, media and entertainment, financial services, consumer packaged goods or CPG, food and beverage, healthcare, and life sciences.

Its primary function is to analyze customer, marketing data, operational efficiency, and sales performance for database preparation through its inference and profiling engine, which eliminates the normally time-consuming process of capturing and organizing data for analysis.

To speed up the exploration and interpretation of data, the solution uses interactive visualizations that allow new questions to be asked to evolve the analyses and conclusions.

3. IBM Watson Analytics.

    The Watson platform is the combination of Artificial Intelligence technology and human language for analyzing huge amounts of data and quickly obtaining answers.

    In the age of digitized information, it is common for exorbitant amounts of information to be generated in the cloud every day, such as posts, photos, formulas, searches, texts, and more. In most cases, this is unstructured data and is therefore not visible to technology and computers.

Figure 15 - IBM Watson Analytics.

And this is where IBM's Watson comes in. Because it is a system based on cognitive computing, it is able to interpret this data, learn from it, and create lines of reasoning from it. It is through this concept that several industries are reinventing themselves with the use of Watson, such as retail, banking, healthcare, and the travel sector, for example.

This IBM product can be easily used even in a small business. With it, the manager has access to advanced business analysis without having knowledge about technical aspects such as data mining, for example.

5.2   18 Tips to Maximize Customer Relationships.

Big Data analytics has the potential to improve various processes in companies. As many of the efforts are directed towards making decisions about strategies and planning to strengthen the relationship with customers, it is important to be aware of these tips.

1º. Predict what customers want.

You can predict what your customers want and always be one step ahead. Yes, this is possible through Big Data actions. There are tools that analyze data related to the behavior of users on your website, for example.

The so-called heat map demonstrates the pages or areas of a website that are most accessed by customers. Thus, if many people access a page of a certain product in an e-commerce, for example, it means that it is something highly searched and that arouses the desire of these people. How about, then, creating a promotion to sell many units of this item? This is using Big Data to anticipate the needs of your customers.

So far, we've talked a lot about customers, but they're not the only people your company can do more accurately with data management.

2nd.   Guide salespeople and the accounting department to visualize real-time data.

The orders placed by the salespeople can always be viewed in real time by the entire team of the company, when using the appropriate management software. This makes sure that inventory write-offs are done correctly.

The other sellers, by monitoring this data, will know when a product is no longer in stock and can no longer be sold, for example. The accounting sector, on the other hand, will have a projection of the amounts that will enter the company's cash.

3rd. Use data to lower operational costs.

If your company notices that customers are no longer interested in a certain type of product, which has seen sales drop, for example, you can suspend the production of that item.

The idea is that operating costs are reduced and that there are no expenses with the production and storage of products that no longer bring the financial return expected by the company.

4th. Incorporate Big Data into customer relationship management.

Big Data plays a key role in customer relationship management. By analyzing large volumes of data, businesses can gain valuable insights into customer behavior, preferences, and needs, allowing for a personalized and targeted approach.

One of the main applications of Big Data in customer relationship management is the personalization of experiences. Based on real-time and historical data, businesses can tailor their offerings, communications, and marketing strategies according to each customer's individual preferences. This creates a more relevant and personalized experience, increasing customer satisfaction and loyalty.

In addition to personalization, Big Data can also be used to identify trends and patterns in customer behavior. Data analysis allows you to identify which products, services, or promotions are most attractive to certain customer segments, helping you make strategic decisions. With this information, businesses can optimize their marketing campaigns and initiatives, directing efforts and resources to the most promising areas.

Another important aspect is the proactive detection of customer issues or dissatisfactions. With real-time data analysis, you can quickly identify negative trends, such as recurring complaints, quality issues, or service failures. This early detection allows companies to take corrective action in an agile way, solving problems before they become more serious and affect the company's image.

In addition, Big Data allows for a better understanding of the customer lifecycle. By analyzing data about the customer journey, from first contact to loyalty, companies can identify the pain points and opportunities for improvement at each stage of the process. This makes it possible to adopt more effective strategies to attract, convert, and retain customers, maximizing the value of the relationship with each of them.

5th. Ensure good communication through various channels.

Contacts with customers, for certain strategies, such as follow-up or post-sales, for example, can be made through various means of communication. E-mail, telephones, social networks, and even written and mailed correspondence, if your audience profile likes this media, can be used.

However, in order for these communications to be made with quality and accuracy, you need to have a solid foundation with all the addresses of your customers. This is only possible with good Big Data management, in which data is always stored and updated frequently.

6th. Analyze your customers' payment preferences.

When a customer makes a purchase, through an e-commerce or even in person at a store, they need to choose a payment method. Thus, if it is noticed that a certain customer prefers to pay with cash instead of a credit card, the company can create exclusive and targeted offers for them.

If it is possible to grant discounts to those who pay in cash and inform these customers of this, the company will certainly have an increase in sales during this period.

7th. Use data to build personas.

The concept of target audience is already somewhat outdated for companies, because, nowadays, the same company can serve several market niches within a large group. Thus, a women's clothing store can cater to both more conservative ladies, and with a classic look, and young women who like to adopt a bolder look, for example.

The ways of approaching these two groups of people cannot be the same, do you agree? Therefore, classifying a target audience only as "women" may not be enough in relationship strategies.

Personas are semi-fictional characters that represent the different customer profiles that a company may have. Within this context, the data collected by Big Data tools can contribute to the construction of these characters and the communication with your customers to be more efficient.

8th. Get to know customers to drive more sales.

When a sale is successfully completed, it is essential for the seller to take the opportunity to collect the customer's data. This valuable information can later be utilized in future negotiations, paving the way for additional sales. However, it's not just about collecting this data, but also about using it strategically to better understand shoppers' behavior.

By carefully analyzing customer data, it is possible to gain valuable insights into their spending habits, preferences, and needs. This in-depth understanding provides a solid foundation for making targeted and personalized approaches, increasing sales effectiveness.

For example, if a specific customer showed interest in sports-related products in their previous purchase, the salesperson can utilize that information when making a new approach. By recommending products or services that are aligned with the customer's interests, the chances of successful sales increase significantly.

In addition, knowing customers also allows you to identify opportunities for cross-selling or upselling. By analyzing buying patterns and complementary products, it is possible to offer the customer related products that can add value to their shopping experience. Not only does this increase the average value of transactions, but it also strengthens customer relationships.

In the financial industry, every sales opportunity is valuable. So, make the most of customer data to understand their needs, anticipate their demands, and offer customized solutions. This proactive and targeted approach will result in an increase in profits and growth for the business.

Keep in mind that the collection of customer data must be done in accordance with applicable privacy and data protection laws. It is critical to ensure the security and confidentiality of customers' personal information while respecting their privacy and obtaining proper consent for the use of their data.

9th. Use data to resolve customer dissatisfaction.

It is already a common practice of modern society to share frustrations on social media. Thus, when a customer is not well served in a commercial establishment or buys a product that they did not like, they can use social networks, such as Facebook and Twitter, as well as complaint sites, such as Reclame Aqui, to vent about their dissatisfaction.

The content of these complaints may also be stored and the information cross-referenced. This cross-referencing can identify what are the main reasons for complaints that customers make on the Internet, enabling possible mistakes made by the company, with regard to the relationship with customers, to be corrected and avoided.

10th.   Employ Big Data in competitor observation.

In the competitive world of business, it is essential to keep a close eye on competitors' actions and strategies. Big Data provides a unique opportunity to collect, analyze, and extract relevant information from large data sets, allowing for detailed observation of the competition.

One of the main advantages of using Big Data in competitor observation is the ability to identify trends and market patterns. By analyzing large volumes of data, it is possible to gain insights into the strategies that are working for competitors, as well as those that are not bringing desirable results. This allows you to adjust your own strategy, based on hard evidence and up-to-date information.

In addition, Big Data can reveal detailed information about competitors' customer behavior. By analyzing data from social networks, transaction records, online surveys, and other sources, it is possible to better understand the profile of the competitor's target audience, their preferences, needs, and expectations. This information can be used to fine-tune your own value proposition and differentiate yourself in the market.

Another benefit of Big Data in competitor observation is the ability to anticipate strategic moves. By analyzing indicators, such as price, product offering, marketing campaigns, and other aspects of competitors' business, you can identify potential opportunities or threats that could affect your own business. This allows you to make more informed decisions and react nimbly to market changes.

However, it is important to point out that Big Data analysis requires technical expertise and appropriate tools. In order to obtain accurate and relevant results, it is necessary to have a robust system for collecting, storing, and analyzing data, as well as skilled professionals to interpret the results and extract meaningful insights.

11th.   Analyze the ROI of digital marketing strategies.

Digital marketing is on the rise and, increasingly, companies use new media to generate leads, that is, arouse interest in people who can become their customers.

This, however, must be done by means of an investment. And to find out if such a cost generated positive results, it is necessary to calculate Return on Investment – ROI.

Big Data can help in this regard, since it is easier to mine conversion data and thus generate the numbers that should be applied in the ROI formula.

12th.   Look for more data sources for marketing actions.

As previously discussed, Big Data contributes to the construction of personas, that is, so that the company can more easily recognize its ideal audience niche. This is also important in marketing actions, since advertising and advertising actions can be more targeted.

To do this, professionals in the sector will be able to search for data so that actions have more results.

In addition, through Big Data tools, it is possible to install automatic data collectors, such as observing the "traces" that customers leave when they access your company's website or blog, for example.

13th.   Study the performance of your competitors.

It is obvious that your competitors will not make confidential company information public, such as financial reports, for example. However, there are some data that can be easily analyzed, such as social media interactions.

If you notice that your competitor ran a marketing campaign on Facebook and got few likes, reactions, and comments on the post, for example, it means that it was not successful. This is important so that you don't do anything similar and analyze what they did wrong.

14º. Practice o benchmarking.

Benchmarking or mystery shopping actions are used to "pluck" information from your competitors. To do this, someone from your company can get in touch with the competition, posing as a customer and, thus, get interesting information, such as the prices practiced and the payment and delivery terms, for example.

All this data needs to be correctly recorded and then analyzed so that it can be compared with the company's reality and develop strategies that make the business a more attractive option for customers.

15º. Analyze competitors' behavior.

It is also important to analyze the behavior of competitors on social networks and other media, such as in advertisements made on television or radio. This is important to understand how the competition's brand positioning generates results for the public, so that it is possible to develop your own identity.

The cross-referencing of interactions that your competitors' customers make on social media is also relevant. This is because, through the identification of the failures committed by these companies, it is possible for your company to act strategically so that customers see your business as a better option in this segment.

16º. A/B test.

A/B tests are comparisons between variables that can be used so that better results are obtained in decision-making. If you have an e-commerce, for example, you can vary the positioning of the products on the site, as well as the colors of the shopping button.

In this way, if you sometimes use a green button, sometimes a red one, and you detect that one of the colors generates more clicks than the other, you can leave the one that presents more results as definitive.

But how do you measure the data from this test? It's simple: through a Big Data tool that records the actions people take on your page.

17th. Practice the pyramid of knowledge technique.

Figure 16 – Knowledge pyramid adapted for Big Data.

The concept of the Pyramid of Knowledge, also called the DIKW Hierarchy, is very relevant for those who seek to develop an organized work with good results. Basically, it is a hierarchical system in which there are four pillars: Data, Information, Knowledge and Wisdom.

Adapted from the concept of the pyramid proposed by Abraham H. Maslow in the 1950s, the knowledge pyramid is a technique that is based on the assumption that the data collected by Big Data tools contribute to decisions being made more assertively and wisely.

The process begins by asking a question that demonstrates a problem that needs to be solved by the company. From this question, you go through the blocks of the pyramid as follows.

Block 1 – Data collection.

Data is qualitative, categorical information. In this block occurs the essential difference of this pyramid in relation to the traditional pyramids of knowledge. Here it is necessary to have Big Data as an objective and collect data from texts, photos, numbers, among other types of data collected that will be complemented with structured databases.

Block 2 – Information.

We can summarize what information is, considering that information is data endowed with relevance and purpose. It has meaning and is organized by some purpose in the company.

In this block, the data collected must be transformed into information, that is, it needs to be interpreted in order to discover what meaning it has.

Block 3 – Knowledge

This is the block in which the Information is used. Knowledge refers to the ability to create a model that describes the object and indicates the actions to be implemented, the decisions to be made.

Based on knowledge, it should be possible to use the information so that informed decisions can be made. The problem raised in step of the question needs to be solved in the best possible way.

Block 4 – Wisdom

Once the problem has been solved, the data can also help the company to act wisely and thus know what the best initiatives are for the future. This means that Big Data can contribute to problems not arising again on other occasions.

18th.   Analyze the data in real time.

Through Big Data, it is possible to track your company's data in real time, and this is important for decision-making. The purpose of this monitoring is to ensure that all the company's decisions are made with a based basis.

Not only big decisions, such as whether or not to make an investment that involves a lot of money, but even simple day-to-day tasks, such as making contact with a customer, can be supported by data.

One of the areas of companies that benefits the most from Big Data is marketing, as all decisions made in this sector must be very strategic.

"What's the difference between Big Data and Hadoop?

Big Data is a large collection of complex and varied data that is difficult to store and analyze using traditional storage methods.

Hadoop is a software framework for storing and processing big data effectively and efficiently."

Roger Magoulas

6   PITFALLS TO AVOID FOR BETTER BIG DATA MANAGEMENT.

Big data management has become increasingly important for businesses across all industries, as the amount of data generated and available today is exponential. However, care must be taken to avoid falling into traps that may compromise the efficiency of this management and, consequently, the results obtained. In this article, I'll cover some of these pitfalls and provide tips for avoiding them.

The lack of proper planning is a common pitfall in big data management and can significantly compromise the results obtained by companies. Many organizations are attracted by the promise of insights and competitive advantages that big data management can offer, and end up diving into data collection without a clear strategy in mind.

Setting objectives and goals is essential for the success of big data management. Without having a clear direction, businesses can end up collecting unnecessary data or getting lost in the vastness of information available. It is crucial to identify the purpose of big data management and how it aligns with the organization's strategic goals. This could include increasing operational efficiency, enhancing the customer experience, identifying market opportunities, or improving decision-making.

In addition to setting objectives, it is important to define success metrics to measure the impact of big data management. These metrics can vary depending on the goals set, and can include indicators such as increased revenue, reduced costs, improved customer satisfaction, or efficiency in data processing. Having clear metrics allows the business to track its progress and assess whether it is achieving the desired results.

Another pitfall related to lack of planning is the lack of an adequate structure for data collection and storage. Big data management involves dealing with large volumes of information coming from a variety of sources. Without proper structure, data can become disorganized, making it difficult to analyze and gain relevant insights. It is necessary to define a data collection system that is efficient and consistent, ensuring the integrity and quality of the data from the moment it is captured.

Additionally, it is essential to have a proper storage and management system in place for the data collected. Choosing a scalable and secure storage infrastructure is critical to handling the massive amount of data generated in the context of big data.

The lack of a robust storage structure can lead to problems such as data loss, poor performance, and difficulties in analyzing data. It is important to invest in suitable storage technologies and solutions, such as NoSQL databases, data warehouses, or cloud storage services, that can handle the scalability and variety of the data.

In addition to proper planning for data collection and storage, it is equally important to consider data governance. Many companies face the challenge of dealing with unstructured, inconsistent, and outdated data.

The lack of proper governance can lead to problems such as data duplication, lack of standardization, and difficulties in identifying data sources. It is critical to establish policies and processes to ensure the quality, integrity, and security of data throughout its lifecycle. This includes defining responsibilities, implementing data cleansing and enrichment practices, standardizing formats, and adopting metadata management techniques.

Another common pitfall is overvaluing the quantity of data at the expense of quality. Too often, companies focus on collecting as much data as possible, but neglect the importance of the relevance and quality of that data. The focus should be on getting the right data that is relevant to the needs of the business. Not all data is equally useful or representative, and analyzing irrelevant or low-quality data can lead to inaccurate results and mistaken conclusions. It is necessary to define clear criteria for the selection and evaluation of data, taking into account their origin, reliability, and relevance to the analyses.

Another pitfall to avoid is the lack of proper control and monitoring of data usage. Big data management involves dealing with sensitive information, such as customers' personal data, financial or strategic company information. It is essential to implement robust security measures to protect this data from unauthorized access, privacy breaches, and cyberattacks.

Additionally, it is important to have control over who has access to the data and how it is used. Lack of proper control and monitoring can lead to misuse of data, violation of data protection regulations, and legal and reputational consequences for the company. It is recommended to implement data access and use policies, defining access permissions based on users' responsibilities and needs, as well as conducting regular audits to ensure compliance and identify any irregularities.

It is essential to establish the purpose of using the data, identify the relevant information to be collected, and determine the metrics that will be used to evaluate the success of the management. Without strategic planning, it's easy to get lost in the plethora of data and not get the results you want.

Another common pitfall is underestimating the importance of data quality. Massive information collection can be impressive, but if the data is inaccurate, incomplete, or outdated, the entire management effort will be in vain. It is essential to invest time and resources in verifying and cleaning data, ensuring its quality before it is used for analysis and decision-making. Additionally, it is important to establish ongoing monitoring processes to ensure that the data remains reliable over time.

One pitfall related to data quality is the lack of integration between different sources of information. Often, companies deal with data coming from several different sources, such as internal systems, social networks, market analysis sites, among others. For efficient big data management, it is necessary to integrate these different data sources, ensuring their coherence and providing a complete view of the available information. Lack of integration can lead to incomplete analyses and erroneous conclusions.

Another pitfall to avoid is the lack of adequate resources for big data management. Processing, storing, and analyzing large volumes of data requires robust infrastructure and efficient systems. It is necessary to invest in the right equipment, technologies, and software solutions to handle the complexity and volume of data. In addition, it is also important to have trained and experienced professionals, such as data scientists and big data engineers, to ensure the correct use and interpretation of data.

Lack of data security is another common pitfall. Big data management involves dealing with sensitive and confidential information, which requires the implementation of robust security measures. This includes the use of encryption, proper access control, monitoring for suspicious activity, and regular backups of the data. A security breach can compromise data integrity, customer privacy, and company reputation, making data protection an absolute priority.

Similarly, the lack of proper governance can also become a trap. It is essential to establish clear policies, guidelines, and processes for the use, access, and sharing of data. This includes defining responsibilities, limiting access to sensitive information, and establishing procedures for the deletion and retention of the data. The absence of governance can lead to decisions based on inconsistent data, lack of compliance with regulations, and even lawsuits.

Finally, it's important to highlight the pitfall of sticking to technology alone. While the implementation of proper technologies is essential for efficient big data management, one cannot neglect the human aspect.

The success of big data management depends as much on the technology as it does on the people involved. It is necessary to empower and educate teams to correctly use data, interpret analyses, and make evidence-based decisions. Cross-functional collaboration and effective communication also play a crucial role in big data management.

So, to avoid the pitfalls of big data management, it's critical to:

1. Conduct strategic planning: Establish clear objectives, identify relevant information, and define success metrics.

2. Ensure data quality: Invest in verifying, cleaning, and monitoring data to ensure

its accuracy and reliability.

3. Integrate different sources of information: Integrate data from diverse sources to get a complete and coherent view of the information available.

4. Have adequate resources: Invest in infrastructure, technologies, and trained professionals to deal with the challenges of big data management.

5. Prioritize data security: Implement robust security measures to protect sensitive and confidential information.

6. Establish proper governance: Set clear policies, guidelines, and processes for the use, access, and sharing of data.

7. Value the human aspect: Empower teams, foster collaboration, and communicate efficiently to ensure effective use of data.

By being aware of these pitfalls and adopting appropriate practices, businesses will be better prepared to get the most value and benefits from big data management. It is worth mentioning that the big data landscape is constantly evolving, and it is important to be up-to-date on new technologies and approaches to ensure increasingly efficient results.

"With data collection, the sooner the better' is always the best answer."

Marissa Mayer[23]

---

[23] Marissa Ann Mayer, born May 30, 1975, is an American businesswoman and investor. She is an information technology executive and co-founder of Sunshine Contact. Mayer previously served as president and CEO of Yahoo!, a position he held in early July 2012.

7   BIG DATA IMPLEMENTATION STRATEGY.

A well-thought-out strategy for the implementation of Big Data is essential for the success of any initiative in this field. Effective implementation of Big Data involves a number of considerations and steps that must be carefully planned and executed. In this article, we will discuss the main aspects of a Big Data implementation strategy.

7.1   Goal Setting.

In defining objectives for the effective implementation of Big Data, it is critical to start with the formulation of clear and specific goals that the organization wants to achieve through this innovative approach.

The breadth of objectives can be varied and adaptable according to the different needs and priorities of the company. From optimizing operational efficiencies to enhancing strategic decision-making capabilities to enhancing personalization of customer service and improving supply chain effectiveness, carefully defining these objectives is crucial to accurately targeting the efforts and resources associated with the use of Big Data.

This initial step not only lays a solid foundation for the successful execution of the strategy, but also opens up the possibility of fully exploiting the transformative potential that Big Data can offer to the organization's operations and bottom line.

7.2   Assessment of Existing Infrastructure.

In assessing the existing infrastructure, there is a crucial need to examine the organization's current technological capability to determine its readiness to deal with Big Data. This process encompasses the thorough analysis of data storage, processing, and analysis capacity, as well as the identification of gaps and areas in need of technological modernization.

If necessary, the implementation of targeted infrastructure investments and the incorporation of appropriate technologies may be considered to strengthen the organization's ability to meet the requirements of Big Data.

This critical step aims to ensure that the infrastructure is aligned with the demands imposed by the effective management of large volumes of data, thereby allowing the organization to fully capitalize on the opportunities offered by this advanced analytics approach.

7.3   Identification of Data Sources.

The subsequent step involves identifying the data sources that are critical to the organization. This process encompasses the collection of both internal data - such as transactions, customer records, and operational information - and external data - such as market data, social media interactions, public information, among others.

The careful identification of these data sources plays a key role in assessing the availability and relevance of information in relation to the objectives determined by the organization.

Not only does this detailed mapping provide valuable insights for strategic planning, but it also guides the fine-grained execution of data analytics initiatives, allowing the organization to maximize the value and usefulness of the available data.

7.4   Selection of Appropriate Technologies.

In the Selection of Appropriate Technologies stage, it is crucial, taking into account the objectives set and the data sources identified, to choose the most appropriate technologies for the processing, storage and analysis of this data.

In this context, there are a range of alternatives available, such as NoSQL databases, data lakes, distributed processing platforms, predictive analytics tools, among others.

The judicious choice of these technologies plays a key role in the effectiveness of

Big Data implementation, allowing for efficient manipulation and valuable insights from the data.

Each selected technology must be aligned with the specific requirements of the organization and the nature of the data to be processed, in order to maximize the potential for value creation and the optimization of data analysis processes.

7.5   Data Collection and Integration.

In the Data Collection and Integration phase, once the technologies have been selected, it becomes necessary to establish effective processes for data collection and integration.

This procedure may involve the implementation of data pipelines, which make it possible to capture and transfer the data to storage and processing systems.

In addition, it is essential to ensure the quality and integrity of data by performing cleansing, transformation, and enrichment steps, preparing it for analysis.

This careful data management not only facilitates the organization and accessibility of relevant data, but also contributes significantly to the accuracy and reliability of the results obtained through Big Data analysis.

Efficient data integration creates a solid foundation for generating insights and making decisions based on strategic, actionable information.

7.6   Analysis and Insight Extraction.

In the Analysis and Insight Extraction stage, which follows the collection and integration of data, the application of various data analysis techniques comes into play, such as machine learning, data mining, and statistics. These techniques are employed with the aim of identifying significant patterns, trends, and correlations in the data collected.

This process makes it possible to extract valuable insights that can support strategic decision-making, identify business opportunities, optimize internal processes, and enhance the customer experience.

In-depth data analysis, combined with the use of advanced tools such as artificial intelligence and predictive analytics, enhances the organization's ability to fully exploit the potential of Big Data, transforming information into results-oriented actions and driving business success.

7.7   Visualization and Communication of Results.

The Visualization and Communication of Results stage plays a crucial role in the effectiveness of Big Data analysis. It is essential to present the insights in a clear and understandable way, making the information accessible and useful to the organization.

Through the use of advanced data visualization techniques, such as graphs, dashboards, and interactive reports, the results of the analysis can be shared in an impactful and meaningful way with work teams, managers, and other stakeholders.

This approach facilitates the understanding of insights and promotes the effective use of information, resulting in strategic decisions based on data and actions guided by the results generated.

Clear and visually appealing communication of results enhances the organization's ability to make the most of the value of the data analyzed, driving innovation, process improvement, and competitive advantage in the marketplace.

7.8   Monitoring and Adjustments.

The Monitoring and Adjustments phase is fundamental in the context of Big Data analysis, as this process is dynamic and requires constant vigilance. It is essential to closely monitor the effectiveness of the models and algorithms employed, identifying potential areas for improvement and necessary adjustments over time.

In addition, monitoring the results after the implementation of the actions is crucial to assess the impact and relevance of the decisions made based on the insights extracted from the analyzed data.

This continuous monitoring allows for an agile response to changes in the business environment and the needs of the organization, ensuring that the effectiveness of Big Data strategies is maintained and the value obtained from data analysis is maximized.

The ability to constantly adjust and optimize analytical approaches contributes significantly to the achievement of established objectives and to continuously improving the organization's processes and results.

7.9   Data Security and Privacy.

With the exponential increase in data collection and processing, data security and privacy have taken on a crucial role. It becomes critical to adopt robust cybersecurity measures, utilize encryption techniques, and implement effective data governance.

These actions aim to ensure the protection of data against threats and breaches, as well as to ensure compliance with applicable data protection laws and regulations.

Protecting the integrity and confidentiality of data is essential for building trust with customers, preserving the company's reputation, and avoiding legal penalties associated with improper handling of sensitive information. By prioritizing data security and privacy, organizations can mitigate significant risks and maintain transparency and accountability in the handling of personal and business data.

7.10 Continuous Improvement.

Continuous improvement in the use of Big Data is essential, as this process is iterative and requires a mindset of constant search for improvements and innovations in data analysis.

Organizations must be ready to adopt new technologies, strengthen staff skills and competencies, and adjust their strategies in response to changes in the business environment and customer demands.

The pursuit of continuous improvement provides a significant competitive advantage, enabling organizations to quickly adapt to market transformations and extract maximum value from the use of Big Data.

By remaining agile and responsive to technological developments and market needs, businesses can drive innovation, optimize processes, and continuously improve their operations to achieve long-term success.

"*Big data analytics is like mining gold in a mine. Only those who are able to extract valuable insights from data have the potential to thrive.*"

Nate Silver[24]

---

[24] American statistician and writer, known for his expertise in data analysis and statistical forecasting. He pioneered the application of statistical techniques and predictive modeling in areas such as politics, sports, and economics.

8   SECURITY, GOVERNANCE, ETHICS AND SOCIETY.

Data security can be thought of as a process of protecting files, databases, and accounts on a network. The system adopts a set of controls, applications, and techniques that identify the relative importance of different data sets, their sensitivity, and regulatory compliance requirements, and then applies appropriate safeguards to protect them.

Governance, in turn, based on the concept of information governance, can be understood as the ability to create a reliable source of information that can be used by employees, partners and customers of the company.

It can be seen that, although data governance and security occupy much of the attention of good companies, it is very likely that they are not prepared for the complexities that are presented by Big Data management.

In general, Big Data analysis is conducted with a wide range of data sources that may not be tested and due to the insecurity generated by this process, companies need to address security and governance policies that apply to this scenario (Ksheri, 2014).

Some of this data will not be necessary and should be properly discarded. The data that remains will need to be protected and governed. Thus, regardless of the company's information management strategy, it needs to have a very well-defined security strategy.

The combination of security and governance will ensure accountability by all parties involved in information management.

Some experts believe that different types of data require different forms of protection, and that in some cases, in a cloud environment, data encryption may in fact be overkill.

It is possible to encrypt everything. An example is writing something to your own hard drive and encrypting it when you send it to your cloud service provider or when you store it in a database provider's cloud. You can encrypt at each layer of the process.

Encrypting everything is a good security alternative, but it represents a loss of performance. For example, many experts advise managing your own keys instead of allowing a cloud provider to do so, and this can become cumbersome. Keeping track of many keys can be a nightmare. In addition, encrypting everything can create other problems.

For example, if your team is trying to encrypt data in a database, you'll need to examine the data as it's stored in the database. This procedure can be expensive and complicated.

Figure 17 – Cyber insecurity.

One of the weaknesses of encryption strategies is that your data is at risk, both before and after it is encrypted. Maintaining a large number of keys can be impractical, and managing key storage, archiving, and access is difficult. To alleviate this problem, generate and compute encryption keys as needed to reduce complexity and improve security.

Here are some other data protection techniques currently available:

- Data anonymization.

    o Data is anonymized when you remove data that can be uniquely linked to an individual, such as a person's name, social security number, or credit card number.

    o Although this technique is very useful to protect personal identification data, generating privacy, it is necessary to be very careful about the amount of information that is removed. If they are insufficient, hackers can still identify who the data refers to.

- Tokenization[25].

    o This technique protects sensitive data by replacing it with random tokens or alias values[26] that mean nothing, to prevent unauthorized people from gaining access to that data.

    o Tokenization can protect credit card information, passwords, personal information, and so on.

    o Some experts argue that it is more secure than encryption.

- Cloud database controls.

    o In this technique, access controls are built into the database to protect the entire database so that it is not necessary to encrypt each segment of data in the cloud.

---

[25] A process that replaces real data with equivalent data of the same format and protected by encryption.

[26] Alias means pseudonym, nickname and, in computing, it is a command that allows you to replace a word with others or with a string.

8.1 Ten Best Practices for Big Data Security

When talking about Big Data security, the focus is invariably on the risks to information protection. This fragility is even greater during the process of deploying Big Data. Big Data projects have received special attention from corporations due to their ability to explore unstructured data in search of new insights and business opportunities.

When working with huge amounts of information from many different sources, you will need to be very careful about security. The storage of the collected data can become a target for virtual attacks and leakage of sensitive information, which would damage the company's reputation, compromising its credibility.

Prioritizing process safety is of utmost importance.

It is necessary to improve the resilience of the systems, using data mirroring and high availability resources, in addition to verifying the regulation and compliance of the storage location, since using Cloud servers makes the management of data security and privacy even more complex (Youself, 2008).

Most of the mistakes made in Big Data projects are related to the lack of authentication mechanisms and the use of channels without security reinforcement to access the database, such as encryption. Thus, in order for the company to remain focused on its Big Data goals and strategies, without having to worry excessively about data security, there are some methods that can minimize these problems.

Here are 10 practices that should be followed:

1º. Monitor the hardware.

The process of collecting the data requires a high level of security, because since it is possible to access information from different sources and different formats, its origins may not be reliable.

Real-time hardware monitoring is required to prevent false data entry and the addition of untrusted devices to a cluster.

To prevent this type of attack, front-end systems such as firewalls[27] and routers should be implemented.

2nd. Ensure the security of data storage and logging.[28]

Storage management is one of the categories that should be most taken into account in security questions. The location of the data is not fixed and can undergo modifications and even malicious attacks.

DRM policy-based encryption29 makes it possible to control content in a restricted manner. Key rotation and transmission encryption are ways to ensure storage protection.

---

[27] A firewall is a network security device that monitors incoming and outgoing network traffic and decides to allow or block specific traffic according to a defined set of security rules.

[28] Data logging is a term used to describe the process of recording relevant events in a computer system.

[29] Digital Restrictions Management – DRM. Rights Management is a technology that aims to protect digital media. Its goal is to curb piracy so that digital content produced by a person or company is not copied and distributed indiscriminately.

If the data is in an untrusted location, it is recommended to use SUNDR30 which increases the chance of detecting unauthorized changes.

3rd. Adopt custom security protocols for NoSQL databases.

The use of NoSQL databases and systems, although it has some benefits, such as cheaper and less laborious scalability, the possibility of using less powerful machines and ease of maintenance, is not considered the safest, as attacks are common.

It is recommended to use secure passwords, hashing algorithms31, and TLS32, which is a security protocol that protects communication between services via the internet, page browsing, and other types of data transfers. In addition, all connections must be logged and data replication must be performed.

4th. Ensure the anonymity of users.

Using anonymized data is not enough to protect the user, as this data can be paired with the owner. Important information is at risk of being leaked, and the professionals who perform the analysis are not always aware of the possible risks (Boyd et al., 2012).

It is recommended that a separation be implemented between the rights and duties of each user, so that each one will be allowed access only to the data

---

[30] Secure Untrusted Data Repository – SUNDR. It is a network file system designed to securely store data on untrusted servers. SUNDR allows clients to detect any attempt at unauthorized modification of files by malicious server operators or users.

[31] A hash function is an algorithm that maps variable-length data to fixed-length data. The values returned by a hash function are called hash values, hash codes, hash sums, checksums, or simply hashes.

[32] Transport Layer Security.

they need to perform their work.

5º. Verify and validate data sources

Perform a complete record of all information to have greater control of the process. Record and control all interactions, ensuring that access is tightly controlled.

To ensure the efficiency of the process and so that data privacy is not compromised, all those that refer to personal identification, registration numbers, among other sensitive information, must be masked or removed (Chen et al., 2017).

In this way, Big Data projects can be customized and have high security capacity so that data is captured and analyzed without any risk to companies.

6º. Certify distributed systems.

Some problems have been recurrent in distributed programming structures, such as information leakage, lack of reliability, and compliance with security policies.

So, the first step is then to establish clear policies and ensure that each node of the distributed structures is secure and has continuous access control.

7º. Validar *Endpoints*[33].

The high frequency of BYOD usage34 has become a major challenge for endpoint validation, as mobile devices can be spoofed, stolen, and even mask users.

It is necessary to strengthen security by using certification and management tools on all devices used.

Control granular access.

Granular access is a method that makes it possible to provide privileges to each user. Each element can be controlled, and some standard practices must be used for this method to be effective.

It is necessary to make sure that this ingress is controlled, maintaining access labels, tracking secrecy requirements from SSO, 35 and developing complete protocols to keep up with restrictions.

8º. Use encryption.

Because big data projects use large streams of data through the cloud, encryption must be a key part of the security process.

Developments in cryptography allow for fully encrypted data calculations, group signature systems that prevent the identification of individuals, and

---

[33] Endpoint security is an approach to protecting a business network, with monitoring status, software, and activities.

[34] Bring Your Own Device – BYOD. Loosely translated, it means bring your own device. This is the concept of the employee using their own equipment, be it a notebook, a tablet or even a smartphone to carry out their professional tasks.

[35] O Single Sign-On – SSO. Single Access is a form of authentication that allows access to different applications and platforms using a single registration. It is a measure widely used in digital media and that streamlines processes for the user experience.

disperse the location of data after each access.

9º. Audit in detail.

Audits must be done granularly, as users often miss or simply ignore security alerts, so auditing needs to be performed regularly to ensure complete protection.

In addition, audit data must be protected to be considered reliable. They must be separated and restricted, and their access must always be logged and controlled.

8.2   Potential risks to society.

Some of the benefits that can emerge from technological progress are clear, but this same technological progress can generate some risks for society. Some forecasts indicate that between the years 2020 and 2060 computing power may surpass human capacity in almost all areas (Helbing, 2015a).

This hypothesis has been a matter of concern for some of the visionaries in the field of technology, experts such as Bill Gates of Microsoft, Elon Musk of Tesla Motors and Apple co-founder Steve Wozniak, as well as physicist Stephen Hawkings point out that over time warnings have been left regarding the negative aspects related to Big Data.

They see computational growth and the volume of data as a problem, because according to these experts, the analysis of human behavior, along the lines of George Orwell's Big Brother, can subject humanity to an even greater danger than that currently represented by nuclear weapons (Helbing et al., 2015a) (Hancock, 2015).

Thinkers such as Helbing (2014) and Chui et al., (2018) go further in this analysis and argue that personalized information[36] builds a bubble around individuals. A kind of digital prison for their thinking, as people are less exposed to other opinions, which can increase polarization within societies and therefore potentiate conflicts.

Creativity and the so-called "thinking outside the box" cannot flow properly, in conditions in which everything that is received in readings, in social networks and in the media is, through the possibilities of selecting the sources available to the subject, the response of himself, that is, of his own ideas.

Personalized information tends to reinforce patterns.

Brundage et al. (2018) call this effect "echo chambers" in which individuals only hear and receive viewpoints that are aligned with their way of thinking or that are aligned with their beliefs.

In short, according to Helbing (2015a) and Pournaras (2015):

> *"A centralized system of technocratic behavioral and social control using a superintelligent system would result in a new form of dictatorship."*

Thus, personalized information, the product so vaunted as the main result of the Big Data universe, can be a double-edged sword, because the same technology can help promote nationalisms, as well as encourage adverse reactions to minorities, give rise to biased election results, etc. (Helbing, 2015b).

These concerns about Big Data are compounded by the fact that much of the type of communication that is carried out within modern societies is mediated to some degree by automated systems (Bollier, 2010).

Brundage et al. (2018) and Acquisti et al. (2015), state that the intrinsic characteristics of Big Data, such as scalability, make it particularly suitable for

---

[36] *Personalized information.*

weakening or distorting public discourse through the production of persuasive content on a large scale, but simultaneously false, which can strengthen despotic regimes on the one hand and undermine the proper functioning of even the most developed democracies on the other.

In short, Big Data is not a technology without possibilities of negative bias, it is not a technology that is above good and evil. There is, then, the emergence and the need to subject this increasingly widespread technology to the values of our societies, that is, to make it compatible with the essential values that govern our societies. Values such as equality, justice, fairness, etc.

According to Helbing (2015a), if this does not occur, sooner or later, technologies will cause significant damage to societies. The author also states that there are reasons to think about the issue more critically, since some countries have already resorted to the use of information to try to manage their societies.

In the 1970s, Chilean President Salvador Allende created computer programs, which included economic models that tried to monitor the performance of the economy in real time, with the aim of improving industrial productivity (Medina, 2011).

As well as the existence of countries such as, for example, Singapore, which uses programs such as Risk Assessment and Horizon Scanning, which is part of the national security coordination center, to help in the administration of society according to the information that is obtained.

The program in question consists of the collection and analysis of large volumes of information, thus allowing an early management of threats to the national integrity of the country, as well as terrorist attacks, infectious diseases and finally the management of financial crises (Kim et al., 2014).

The willingness on the part of other countries to emulate the model in question potentiates the most critical opinions.

In general, the risks related to the social good are quite similar to those for more routine uses. One of the biggest risks is that Big Data tools and techniques can be misused by authorities and others with access to them (Michael et al., 2018).

Exemplifying the above point of view, we have the conduct of the Chinese government that has been exploring ways to obtain information online and offline to assign a score to its citizens (citizen score). This score varies between 350 and 950 points when it is associated with costs and benefits.

For example, a citizen who has a score that exceeds 700 can apply for a travel visa to Singapore by not submitting some documents, in order to speed up the process. However, in the event of conduct deemed inappropriate, citizens may suffer costs such as being prevented from obtaining a travel visa.

However, if, on the one hand, some aspects of situations such as those mentioned in the previous paragraphs, on the other hand, the ambiguity remains, the following thought exposed below by Chen and Cheung (2017, p.357) allows us to better understand this relationship:

> "They're unsure about what contributes to their social credit scores, how those scores are matched with the state system, and how their data is interpreted and used. In short, Big Data-based scoring is putting Chinese citizens in front of major challenges regarding privacy and personal data."

Several entities disagree with this practice. For example, according to the European Group on Ethics in Science and New Technologies, the improvement of social processes based on Big Data resources that involve social scoring systems violates fundamental ideas such as equality and freedom.

The system, instead of considering the different characteristics of people, creates different types of people similar to caste systems.

As well as, according to Michael et al. (2018) and Helbing et al. (2015b), the widespread use of censorship in China more explicitly exemplifies how technology can be instrumentalized for political purposes in authoritarian states.

The pendulum of intentions behind the motivations that underpin Big Data swings both ways, that is, it can be effectively good, because it is hoped that the scoring system can improve public management, demanding more coherence in the activities carried out and ultimately providing more equality.

As there is no consensus regarding the nature of Big Data, some authors and personalities in the technology area express great concern about the possible less positive contours that it may assume in the future, others go in exactly the opposite direction.

Experts opposed to the expansion of Big Data believe that the debate on the analysis of data that travels on the internet should stick to the commercial context so that society is not distorted (AlgorithmWatch, 2019).

However, regardless of the ambiguities that exist, there is a consensus that citizens should be educated and/or equipped with tools and knowledge that allow them to navigate more smoothly in this new scenario created by the technologies in question.

In addition to government programs that process circulating data to censor or manipulate citizens, there is another ethical issue that can be generated by Big Data: the loss of privacy.

Activities that were only in the inner circle or shared only with a few individuals close to the subjects, now when performed in the digital world, leave very revealing clues, as they unveil their interests, inform about personality traits, beliefs, as well as what their possible intentions are.

Dealing with this problem becomes equally important because, according to Acquisti et al., (2015), the erosion of privacy can threaten the autonomy of everyone, not only as consumers, but also as citizens.

While there is a frantic race to obtain ever-increasing amounts of data, it is important to keep in mind that more data does not necessarily translate into advances or progress, nor into better social conditions.

We are increasingly dependent on information technologies. They are increasingly present in all segments of our lives, whether on a personal or professional level. Control over personal data has become an issue inherently linked to issues of personal choice, autonomy, and socioeconomic power.

Privacy-related dilemmas pose a major challenge today. And this challenge is only going to grow.

8.3   Big Data Regulation.

Regulation can play an important role in ensuring that markets function properly (Gov.Uk, 2015). However, the whole context of Big Data is quite new and permeated by volatilities and the fact that there remains a certain lack of knowledge in this area leads the institutions that manage free competition and market regulations to proceed with caution when it comes to the challenges imposed by Big Data.

It is necessary for society to become aware that Big Data not only challenges existing regulatory instruments, but that it will force authorities to create control instruments, as society itself is adapting to it (Hamad, 2015).

At the same time, some studies indicate that the implementation of strict regimes aimed at ensuring the protection of privacy can create distortions in the markets, as they reduce the potential of the target consumers to analyze and therefore hinder the development of internet commerce. Innovation can also be hindered (Acquisti et al., 2016).

However, despite the challenges posed by Big Data, countries have not been indifferent to such dilemmas, although they are somewhat dissonant in the actions they have been taking.

The EU[37] has been striving to create barriers to prevent the misuse of information, as well as to prevent the inappropriate use of it. It has strengthened its position in

---

[37] European Union.

regulating this issue, since after four years of negotiations it adopted the GDPR[38] on April 14, 2016.

The regulation brings significant changes to the protection of EU citizens' personal data and goes further than standardising national data protection laws across the EU. It introduces important principles, such as requiring explicit consent from consumers so that information about them can be used by businesses, as well as the right to be forgotten which is considered one of the most demanding principles that the regulation imposes on businesses.

Figure 18 – GDPR.

The GDPR also introduces:

- Data portability.

  The act of transferring data from one company to another, at the request of the data subject. Thus, if an individual wishes to change the provider of a service or product, they simply request portability and the company will have to transfer their personal data to another.

- Data protection by design.

---

[38] General Data Protection Regulation – GDPR. It is an EU Regulation of 2016/679 of the European Parliament and of the Council of 27 April 2016 on the protection of natural persons with regard to the processing of personal data and on the free movement of such data.

The concept of Privacy by Design emerged in the 1990s and is currently incorporated into data protection law. That is why it is so important that there are secure and transparent means of data collection and processing. In this way, both parties guarantee the security and privacy of information.

- A figura do data protection officer.

    It is an entity that will have to be designated by companies to ensure the protection of individuals' information, as well as to ensure that the procedures required by the GDPR are complied with by the company to which it belongs.

    The figure in question comes into play when companies start to have large volumes of data in their processes or when the information in question is sensitive, as is the case with information from sectors such as health and finance.

The GDPR is automatically accepted in the legal systems of all EU member countries and is mandatory. It provides for the application of fines that can reach 20 million euros and 4% of the total turnover of companies in case of harmful behavior to citizens.

In Brazil, the General Law for the Protection of Personal Data, LGPD, Law No. 13,709, of August 14, 2018, provides for the processing of personal data, including in digital media, by a natural person or by a legal entity under public or private law, with the aim of protecting the fundamental rights of freedom and privacy and the free development of the personality of the natural person.

The LGPD is the first legislation in Brazil that specifically addresses the use of personal data. In the case of the European Union, this issue already found legal support approximately 25 years ago in Directive 95/46/EC.

Figure 19 – LGPD.

Therefore, it is not surprising that the discussions of the European model are well matured and, in this way, it serves as a model for several countries, including Brazil.

Many multinational companies, which have already gone through the race to comply with the GDPR, may have the false impression that they are already prepared to deal with the requirements of Brazilian law.

It is also important to note that the GPDR is a regulation and, therefore, seeks to be more direct and objective in its terms, establishing specific rules for different situations.

The LGPD, on the other hand, is a law, with more open and subjective clauses, allowing different interpretations on some points, which will be consolidated by jurisprudence and regulated by the ANPD, once created.

Despite this, both have the same objective: to ensure the privacy of individuals and, indirectly, to call on companies to face the problem of **information** security.

9   LGPD vs. RGPD.

Several similarities between LGPD and GDPR can be listed, but there are specific characteristics and approaches, in each of the instruments, that require a lot of attention in order not to commit any infringement. Listed here are the main points.

9.1   Territorial scope.

The GDPR and LGPD have similar territorial scopes: they are applicable to all companies that offer goods or services to citizens in the European Union or Brazil, respectively, regardless of where they are located.

However, the LGPD claims broad applicability, even outside Brazil, in provisions that may be even more extensive than those of the GDPR.

As provided in the text of the LGPD, it applies to any processing:

- Carried out in the national territory, that is, in Brazil.

- Associated with the offer of goods or services in the national territory or involving personal data of individuals located in the national territory.

- Personal data collected in the national territory.

As with the GDPR, this broad scope applies to processing activities that take place entirely outside of Brazil but affect or target Brazilian citizens.

Both the GDPR and the LGPD qualify consent as the key element for companies to process personal data.

9.2   Legal Bases for Data Processing.

Similarly, LGPD and GDPR recognize legal bases for the processing of personal data.

In general, the GDPR considers:

- Explicit consent.

- Contractual necessity.

- Execution of public policies.

- Interest vital.

- Legal obligation.

- Legitimate interest.

The LGPD adopts the six provisions of the GDPR and adds some more specific ones, namely:

- The protection of health in a procedure performed by health professionals.

- Conducting studies by a research body.

- Exercise of rights in legal proceedings.

- Credit protection.

9.3 Data Subject Access Requests

Both the LGPD and the GDPR guarantee the individual the right to access their personal data.

Likewise, data subjects may, at any time, request that the companies that collected their data carry out the portability, correction or definitive deletion of their information.

The difference, in this regard, is in the deadline set for companies to offer access. While the GDPR states that companies have 30 days to respond to requests, the LGPD offers only 15 days.

9.4 Direct Marketing

Another major difference between the LGPD and the GDPR concerns the processing of personal data for direct marketing purposes. The European regulation defines the specific requirements and steps to be followed in these cases, while the Brazilian law does not directly address the matter.

The GDPR grants data subjects the right to object, at any time, to the processing of their personal data for profiling and marketing purposes.

The LGPD, on the other hand, does not specifically address direct marketing and this may suggest implicit authorization, as long as the processing follows the general rules applicable to consent, transparency, and the rights of data subjects.

9.5   Data breach notifications.

The LGPD does not have detailed deadlines for reporting data leakage to the supervisory authority. The law only says that the communication must be made within a "reasonable" time.

The GDPR, on the other hand, states that these incidents must be notified within 72 hours.

On the other hand, Brazilian law also mandates that individuals who have their data breached are also notified of the incident, which is not a requirement in the European regulation.

9.6   Sanctions.

The penalties to which companies are subject follow the same approach.

The GDPR states that in the event of a data breach incident, there may be fines ranging from 10 to 20 million Euros or from 2% to 4% of the total annual turnover of the previous financial year, whichever is greater.

The LGPD, in turn, establishes simple fines of up to 2% of the previous year's global revenue up to 50 million reais per violation.

It is also important to note that the GPDR is a regulation and, therefore, seeks to be more direct and objective in its terms, establishing specific rules for different situations.

The LGPD, on the other hand, is a law, with more open and subjective clauses, allowing different interpretations on some points, which will be consolidated by jurisprudence and regulated by the ANPD, once created.

Despite this, both have the same objective: to guarantee the privacy of individuals and, indirectly, to call on companies to face the problem of **information** security.

"Big data analytics is changing the way businesses operate and how society works. It's a new industrial revolution."

Eric Brynjolfsson[39]

---

[39] Professor and researcher of digital economy.

10   ACRONYMS.

ACID - Atomicity, Consistency, Isolation, Durability.

AI – Artificial intelligence.

API - Application Programming Interface.

AWS – Amazon Web Services.

BDL - Bayesian Deep Learning.

BGaaS – Big Data as a Service.

BI – Business Intelligence.

BSON - Binary JSON.

BYOD - Bring Your Own Device.

CEO – Chief Executive Officer.

CEP - Complex Event Processing.

CMDB - Configuration Management Database.

COBIT – Control Objectives for Information and Related Technology.

CPU - Central Processing Unity.

CQL - Cassandra Query Language.

CRM - Customer Relationship Management.

CSP – Cloud Service Provider.

CSV – Comma Separated Values.

DARPA - Defense Advanced Research Projects Agency.

DBA – Database Administrator.

DBMS - Database Management System.

DER – Diagram of Entities and Relationships.

DRM - Digital Restrictions Management.

DSR – Design Science Research.

DW – Data Warehouse.

ERP – Enterprise Resource Planning.

ETL - Extract, transform and Load.

EU – European Union.

GIS - Geographic Information System.

GNU - General Public License.

GQM – Goal Question Metric.

HDFS – Hadoop Distributed File System.

HFT - High Frequency Trading.

HTTPS - Hyper Text Transfer Protocol Secure.

AI - Artificial Intelligence.

IaaS - Infrastructure as a Service.

IBM – International Business Machines Corporation.

IDC - International Data Corporation.

IP – Internet Protocol.

ISO - International Organization for Standardization.

ITIL – Information Technology Infrastructure Library.

JSDL – Job Submission Description Language.

JSON - JavaScript Object Notation.

KPI - Key Performance Indicators.

LAMP - Linux, Apache, Mysql, PHP, Perl or Python.

LDAP – Lightweight Directory Access Protocol.

LGPD – General Personal Data Protection Law.

MDM - Mobile Device Management.

MER. Entity and Relationship Model.

MOM - Message Oriented Middleware.

NIST – National Institute Standards and Technology.

NLP - Natural Language Processing.

NoSQL – Not Only Structured Query Language.

ODBC – Open Data Base Connectivity.

OGC - Open Geospatial Consortium.

OWL - Web Ontology Language.

P2P - Peer-to-peer.

PaaS – Platform as a Service.

PBS – Product Breakdown Structure.

PC – Private Cloud.

PC – Public Cloud.

RAM – Random Access Memory.

RDF - Resource Description Framework.

REST - Representational State Transfer.

RFID - Radio Frequency IDentification.

GDPR - General Data Protection Regulation.

ROI - Return on Investiment.

RPC - Remote Procedure Call.

SaaS – Software as a Service.

DBMS - Database Management System.

SI – Information System.

SLA – Service Level Agreement.

SOA – Service Oriented Architecture.

SOAP - Simple Object Access Protocol.

SPI - Service Provider Infrastructure.

SQL – Structured Query Language.

SRI - Information Retrieval System.

SSL - Secure Sockets Layer.

SSO – Single Sign On.

SUNDR - Secure Untrusted Data Repository.

TCP - Transmission Control Protocol.

IT – Information Technologies.

TLS - Transport Layer Security.

TQM - Total Quality Management.

UCP - Central Processing Unity.

UDF – User Defined Function.

UML - Unified Modeling Language.

VM - Virtual Machine.

VMM - Virtual Monitor Machine.

VPN – Virtual Private Network.

VSAM – Virtual Storage Access Method.

WBS - Work Breakdown Structure.

WSLA – Web Service Agreement Language.

XAI - Explainable Artificial Intelligence

XML - Extensible Markup Language.

XSLT - eXtensible Stylesheet Language Transformation.

XSS - Cross-Site Scripting.

YARN - Yet Another Resource Negotiator.

Figure 20 – Is it complicated to implement Big Data?

11   REFERENCES.

ACQUISTI, A., BRANDIMARTE, L., & LOEWENSTEIN, G. (2015). Privacy and human behavior in the age of information. Science, 347(6221), 509-514. Disponível em: https://www.heinz.cmu.edu/~acquisti/papers/Acquisti-Science-Privacy-Review.pdf.

ACQUISTI, A., TAYLOR, C., & WAGMAN, L. (2016). The economics of privacy. Journal of Economic Literature, 54(2), 442-92.

ACQUISTI, A., TAYLOR, C., & WAGMAN, L. (2016). The economics of privacy. Journal of Economic Literature, 54(2), 442-92.

AKIDAU, Tyler, CHERNYAK, Slava, LAX, Reuven. (2019). Streaming Systems: The What, Where, When, and How of Large-Scale Data Processing.

ALGORITHMWATCH. (2019) Automating Society 2019. Available at: https://algorithmwatch.org/en/automating-society-2019/

ANDERLA, G. (1979). The information in 1985. Rio de Janeiro: CNPq/IBICT, 1979.

ARAUJO, V.M.R.H. de. (1995) Information Systems: A New Conceptual Theoretical Approach. Journal of Information Science, v. 24, n. 1, p. 37-44.

ARMSTRONG, M. (2006). Competition in two-sided markets. The RAND Journal of Economics.

ARMSTRONG, M. (2006). Competition in two-sided markets. The RAND Journal of Economics, 37(3), 668-691.

BELKIN, N.J. (1978). Information concepts for information science. Journal of Documentation, v. 34, n. 1, p. 55-85.

BELKIN, N.J., ROBERTSON, S.E. (1976) Information science and the phenomenon of information. Jasis, v.27, n.4, p.197-204.

BOLLIER, D., & Firestone, C. M. (2010). The promise and peril of Big Data.

Washington, DC: Aspen Institute, Communications and Society Program.

BOYD, D; CRAWFORD, K. (2012). Critical Questions for Big Data: Provocations for a Cultural, Technological, and Scholarly Phenomenon. Information, Communication, & Society v.15, n.5, p. 662-679.

BRETON, P. & PROULX, S. (1989). The explosion of communication. the birth of a new ideology. Paris: La Découverte.

BUBENKO, J. A., WANGLER, B. (1993). "Objectives Driven Capture of Business Rules and of Information System Requirements". IEEE Systems Man and Cybernetics'93 Conference, Le Touquet, France.

BUSINESSWIRE. (2019). MicroStrategy Announces Top 10 Enterprise Analytics Trends to Watch in 2020 Report. Disponível em: https://www.businesswire.com/news/home/20191212005348/en/MicroStrat egy-Announces-Top-10-Enterprise-Analytics- Trends#:~:text=%20MicroStrategy%20Announces%20Top%2010%20Enterpris e%20Analytics%20Trends,%205%20Next- Gen%20Embedded%20Analytics%20Speeds...%20More%20.

CHEN, H., CHIANG, R. H., & STOREY, V. C. (2012). Business Intelligence and Analytics: From Big Data to Big Impact. MIS Quarterly.

CHEN, Y., & CHEUNG, A. S. (2017). The transparent self under Big Data profiling: privacy and Chinese legislation on the social credit system. Disponível em: https://papers.ssrn.com/sol3/papers.cfm?abstract_id=2992537 Mar.2019).

CHENG, Y., Qin, c., & RUSU, F. (2012). Big Data Analytics made easy. SIGMOD '12 Proceedings of the 2012 ACM SIGMOD International Conference on Management of Data New York.

CHUI, M., HARRYSON, M., MANYIKA, J., ROBERTS, R., CHUNG, R., HETEREN,V.A., NEL, P. (2018). Notes from the AI frontier: Applying AI for social good. Disponível em: https://www.mckinsey.com/~/media/McKinsey/Featured%20Insights/Artificia l%20Intelligence/Applying%20artificial%20intelligence%20for%20social%20go od/MGI-Applying-AI-for-social-good-Discussion-paper-Dec-2018.ashx.

CODD, E.F., 1970. "A Relational Model for Large Shared Databanks". Communications of the ACM (Jun), 13(6), pp. 377-387.

COHEN, Reuven. (2012). Brazil's Booming Business of Big Data – Disponível em: https://www.forbes.com/sites/reuvencohen/2012/12/12/brazils-booming-business-of-bigdata/?sh=1de7e6bc4682

COMPUTERWORLD. (2016) Ten cases of Big Data that guaranteed a significant return on investment. Available at: https://computerworld.com.br/plataformas/10-casos-de-big-data-que-garantiram-expressivo-retorno-sobre-investimento/.

DAVENPORT, T. H. (2014). Big Data at Work: Debunking Myths and Uncovering Opportunities. Rio de Janeiro: Elsevier.

DAVENPORT, T; PATIL, D. (2012). Data scientist: the sexiest job of the 21st century. Harvard Business Review. Disponível em: https://hbr.org/2012/10/data-scientist-the-sexiest-job-of-the-21st-century.

DAVENPORT, T; PATIL, D. (2012). Data scientist: the sexiest job of the 21st century. Harvard Business Review. Disponível em: https://hbr.org/2012/10/data-scientist-the-sexiest-job-of-the-21st-century.

DAVIS, A., 1992. "Operational Prototyping: A New Development Approach". IEEE Software (Sep/Oct).

DIXON, James. 2010. Pentaho, Hadoop, and Data Lakes. Blog, October. Disponível em: https://jamesdixon.wordpress.com/2010/10/14/pentaho-hadoop-and-data-lakes/

EDWARD Choi, M. T. (2017). RETAIN: An Interpretable Predictive Model for Healthcare using Reverse Time Attention Mechanism. Disponível em https://arxiv.org/pdf/1608.05745.pdf

ELMASRI, R.; WUU, Gene T. J.; KORAMAJIAN, Vram. 1993. A Temporal Model and Query Language for EER Databases. In: Tansel, A. et al. Temporal Databases:

theory, designs and implementation. Redwood City: The Benjamim/Cummings Publishing, p.212-229.

FORBES. (2012) Available at: https://www.forbes.com/sites/reuvencohen/2012/12/12/brazils-booming-business-of-bigdata/?sh=1de7e6bc4682

FRANCIS, L. (2009). Cloud Computing: Implications for Enterprise Software Vendors (ESV), System Design and Management Program. Massachusetts Institute of Technology.

FRANCIS, L. (2009). Cloud Computing: Implications for Enterprise Software Vendors (ESV),System Design and Management Program. Massachusetts Institute of Technology.

GENS, Frank. IDC Predictions 2012: Competing for 2020. IDC (Dezembro de 2011). http://cdn.idc.com/research/Predictions12/Main/downloads/ IDCTOP10Predictions2012.pdf

GLASS, R. ; CALLAHAN, (2015).S. The Big Data-Driven Business: How to Use Big Data to Win Customers, Beat Competitors, and Boost Profit. New Jersey: John Wiley & Sons, Inc.

GLASS, R., CALLAHAN, (2015). S. The Big Data-Driven Business: How to Use Big Data to Win Customers, Beat Competitors, and Boost Profit. New Jersey: John Wiley & Sons, Inc.

GÓMEZ-BARROSO, J. L. (2018). Experiments on personal information disclosure: Past and future avenues. Telematics and Informatics, 35(5), 1473-1490.Disponível em: https://doi.org/10.1016/j.tele.2018.03.017

GOV.UK. (2015). The commercial use of consumer data: Report on CMA´S call for information. Disponível em: https://assets.publishing.service.gov.uk/government/uploads/system/uploads /attachment_dat a/file/435817/The_commercial_use_of_consumer_data.pdf.

GUALTIERI, M. (2013). Big Data Predictive Analytics Solutions. Massachusetts:

Forrester.

GUALTIERI, M. (2013). Big Data Predictive Analytics Solutions. Massachusetts: Forrester.

GUOLINAG, L., BENG, C. O., JIANHUA, F., Jianyoung, W., & Lizhu, Z. (2008). EASE: an effective 3-in-1 keyword search method for unstructured, semi-structured and structured data. SIGMOD '08 Proceedings of the 2008 ACM SIGMOD International Conference on Management of data, pp. 903-914.

HALPER, F. (2013). How To Gain Insight From Text. TDWI Checklist Report.

HALPER, F. (2014). Demystifying Cloud BI. TDWI Checklist Report.

HALPER, F. (September de 2013). How To Gain Insight From Text. TDWI Checklist Report.

HALPER, F., & KRISHNAN, K. (2013). TDWI Big Data Maturity Model Guide Interpreting Your Assessment Score. TDWI Benchmark Guide 2013–2014.

HAMAD, R. et al. Using "Big Data" to Capture Overall Health Status: Properties and Predictive Value of a Claims-Based Health Risk Score. Cambridge: Plos One, 2015

HANCOCK, Jeff T. (2015). The Facebook Study: A Personal Account of Data Science, Ethics and Change. In: Proceedings of the 18th ACM Conference on Computer Supported Cooperative Work & Social Computing. ACM, p. 1. Disponível em: https://dl.acm.org/doi/10.1145/2675133.2697078.

HELBIG C, RINK K, Marx A, PRIESS J, FRANK M, KOLDITZ O (2012) Visual integration of diverse environmental data : a case study in Central Germany. In: Proceedings of iEMSs Conference 2012, Leipzig, Germany, pp 1–8

HELBING, D. (2014). The World after Big Data: What the Digital Revolution Means for Us. Disponível em: http://papers.ssrn.com/sol3/papers.cfm?abstract_id=2438957.

HELBING, D. (2015a). Big Data Society: Age of Reputation or Age of

Discrimination?. In: HELBING, D. Thinking Ahead-Essays on Big Data, Digital Revolution, and Participatory Market Society. Springer International Publishing. p. 103-114.

HELBING, D. (2015b). Thinking Ahead-Essays on Big Data, Digital Revolution, and Participatory Market Society. Springer International Publishing.

HILBERT, M. (2013). Big Data for Development: From Information to Knowledge Societies. Disponível em https://www.researchgate.net/publication/254950835_Big_Data_for_Development_From_Information-_to_Knowledge_Societies.

IBM. (2014). Exploiting Big Data in telecommunications to increase revenue, reduce customer churn and operating costs. Fonte: IBM: http://www-01.ibm.com/software/data/bigdata/industry-telco.html.

INMON, W. H. (1992). Building the Data Warehouse. John Wiley & Sons, New Yorkm NY, USA.

INMON, W. H. (1996). Building the Data Warehouse. John Wiley & Sons, New Yorkm NY, USA.2nd edition.

JARVELIN, K. & Vakkari, P. (1993) The evolution of Library and Information Science 1965-1985: a content analysis of journal articles. Information Processing & Management, v.29, n.1, p. 129-144.

KAMIOKA, T; TAPANAINEN, T. (2014). Organizational use of Big Data and competitive advantage - Exploration of Antecedents. Disponível em: https://www.researchgate.net/publication/284551664_Organizational_Use_of_Big_Data_and_Competitive_Advantage_-_Exploration_of_Antecedents.

KANDALKAR, N.A; WADHE, A. (2014). Extracting Large Data using Big Data Mining, International Journal of Engineering Trends and Technology. v. 9, n.11, p.576-582.

KANDALKAR, N.A; WADHE, A. Extracting Large Data using Big Data Mining, International Journal of Engineering Trends and Technology. v. 9, n.11, p.576-

582. 2014

KIMBALL, R.; ROSS, M. (2013). The Data Warehouse Toolkit: The Definitive Guide to Dimensional Modeling, Third Edition. Wiley 10475 Crosspoint Boulevard Indianapolis, IN 46256: John Wiley & Sons, Inc.

KIMBALL, R., THORNTHWAITE, W., REEVES, L., ROSS, M., (1998b). The Data Warehouse Lifecycle Toolkit: Expert Methods for Designing, Developing and Deploying Data Warehouses. New York, John Wiley & Sons.

KIMBALL, Ralph; et al. (1998a). The Data Warehouse Lifecycle Toolkit: expert methods for designing, developing, and deploying Data Warehouses. New York: John Wiley & Sons. 771p.

KSHETRI, N. (2014). Big Data' s impact on privacy, security and consumer welfare. Telecommunications Policy, 38 (11), 1134-1145.

KSHETRI, N. (2014). Big Data' s impact on privacy, security and consumer welfare. Telecommunications Policy, 38 (11), 1134-1145.

LAVALLE, S., LESSER, E., SHOCKLEY, R., HOPKINS, M. S., & KRUSCHWITZ, N. (2010). Big Data, Analytics and the Path From Insights to Value.

LOHR, S. (2012). The Age of Big Data. The New York Times.

MACHADO, Felipe Nery Rodrigues. 2018. Database-Design and Implementation. [S.l.]: Editora Saraiva.

MANYIKA, J. (2011). Big Data: The next frontier for innovation, competition, and productivity. Disponível em: https://www.semanticscholar.org/paper/Big-data%3A-The-next-frontier-for-innovation%2C-and-Manyika/91b63db746becca15090963a8990dfe2b5103799.

MANYIKA, J., CHUI, M., BROWN, B., BUGHIN, J., DOBBS, R., ROXBURGH, C., & BYERS, A. H. (2011). Big Data: The next frontier for innovation, competition, and productivity.

MCAFFE, A., & BRYNJOLFSSON, E. (2012). Big Data: The Management Revolution.

Harvard Business Review. Disponível em Harvard Business
Review: http://www.forbes.com/sites/gartnergroup/2013/03/27/gartners-
big-data-definition-consistsof-three-parts-not-to-be-confused-with-three-vs/.

MEDINA, E. (2011). Cybernetic revolutionaries: Technology and politics in Allende's
Chile. Mit Press.

MOHANIA, M., SAMTANI, S., RODDICK, J., KAMBAYASHI, Y.. (1999. "Advances and
Research Directions in Data Warehousing Technology". Research Report
ACRC-99-006, School of Computer and Information Science, University of
South Australia.

OHLHORST, J. F. (2012). Big Data Analytics: Turning Big Data into Big Money. Wiley.

OSWALDO, T., PJOTR, P., MARC, S., & RITSERT, C. J. (2011). Big Data, but are we
ready? Disponível em: https://www.nature.com/articles/nrg2857-c1.

PAVLO, A., PAULSON, E., RASIN, A., ABADI, D. J., DEWITT, D. J., MADDEN, S., &
STONEBRAKER, M. (2009). A comparison of approaches to large-scale data
analysis. SIGMOD, pp. 165–178.

PERSIVAL, I. (1992). Chaos: a science for the real world. In: Hall, N. (ed.) The new
scientist guide to chaos. London: Penguin Books

POHL, K., 1993. "The Three Dimensions of Requirements Engineering". In: Rolland
C., Bodart F., Cauvet C. (eds.) 5th International Conference on Advanced
Information Systems Engineering (CAiSE'93), Springer-Verlag, Paris, pp. 275-
292

PUTRI, N. R., & MGANGA, M. C. (2011). Enhancing information in cloud computing
services using sla based metrics. Master's thesis, School Computing. Blekinge
Institute of Technology.

Qi, Z., Lu, C., & RAOUF, B. (2010). Cloud Computing state of the art and research
challanges. Cloud Computing state of the art and research challanges, pp. 7 -
18.

QIN, H. F., & LI, Z. H. (2013). Research on the Method of Big Data Analysis. 2013

Asian Notwork for Scientific Information, pp. 1-7.

RAJ, P., & DEKA, G. C. (2012). Handbook of Research on Cloud Infrastructures for Big DataAnalytics. Information Science: IGI Global.

ROGERS, S. (2010). Information is power. Disponível em The Guardian: http://www.theguardian.com/media/2010/may/24/data-journalism.

RUSSOM, P. (2011). Big Data Analytics. TDWI Best Practices Report Fourth Quarter 2011: Big Data Analytics.

SAGAN, Carl. (1985). The Dragons of Eden. Publisher Círculo do Livro.

SHERA, J. H. & Cleveland, D. B. (1977). History and foundations of Information Science. Annual Review of Information Science and Technology, v. 12, p.248-275.

SILVA, C. A., FERREIRA, A. S., & GEUS, P. L. (2012). A methodology. Proceedings of the IEEE Latin American Conference on Cloud Computing and Communications, LatinCloud'12 (p. for management of cloud computing using security criteria). Porto, Alegre, Brazil: IEEE Latin American Conference on Cloud Computing and Communications.

SOMMERVILLE, I., 2007. Software Engineering. Eigth Edition, Addison Wesley.

STONEBRAKER, M. (2012). What Does 'Big Data' Mean? What Does 'Big Data' Mean? | blog@CACM | Communications of the ACM.

STUBBS, E. (2014). Big Data, Big Innovation: Enabling Competitive Differentiation through Business Analytics. John Wiley & Sons.

SUBRAMANIAM, Anushree. 2020. What is Big Data? – A Beginner's Guide to the World of Big Data. Disponível em: edureka.co/blog/what-is-big-data/.

TANKARD, C. (2012). Big Data security, Network Security, Volume 2012, Issue7, July 2012, Pages 5 -8, ISSN 1353-4858.

TAURION, C. (2013). Interview with Cezar Taurion: The current stage of Big Data in Brazil. Available on IBM: https://www.ibm.com/developerworks/community/blogs/bigdata/entry/entrevista_com_cezar_taurion_o_estagio_atual_do_big_data_no_brasil?lang=en.

TM FORUM. (2005). Sla management handbook - volume 2. Technical Report GB9712, TeleManagement Forum.

TM FORUM. (2005). Sla management handbook - volume 2. Technical Report GB9712, TeleManagement Forum.

VAISHNAVI, V. K., & KUECHLER, W. (2004). Design Science Research in Information Systems.

VAN AALST, W. M., VAN HEE, K. M., VAN WERF, J. M., & VERDONK, M. (March de 2010). Auditing 2.0: Using Process Mining to Support Tomorrow's Auditor. Computer (Volume:43, Issue:3.

VAQUERO, L. M., Merino, L. R., Caceres, J., & Lindner, M. (2009). A break in the clouds: towards a cloud definition. ACM SIGCOMM Computer Communication Review, pp. 50-55.

WANG, Y., KUNG, L., & BYRD, T. A. (2018). Big Data analytics: Understanding its capabilities and potential benefits for healthcare organizations. Technological Forecasting and Social Change, 126, 3-13.

WASNIOWSKI, R. A. (2014). A Cloud Oriented Framework for Scientific Data Processing.

WEBSTER, J., & WATSON, R. T. (2002). Analysing The Past to Prepare for the Future: Writing a Literature Review.

WIDJAYA, Ivan. (2019). WHAT ARE THE COSTS OF BIG DATA? Disponível em: http://www.smbceo.com/2019/09/04/what-are-the-costs-of-big-data/

YANG, F., SHANMUGASUNDARAM, J., & YERNENI, R. (2009). A scalable data platform for a large number of small applications. CIDR.

YOON, J. P. (2011). Access Control And Trustiness for Resource Management in Cloud Databases. Springer.

YOUSEFF, L., BUTRICO, M., & DA SILVA, D. (2008). Toward a Unified Ontology of Cloud Computing. Grid. GCE'08.

YU, E., 1995. "Modelling Strategic Relationships for Process Reengineering". Phd Thesis, University of Toronto.

YUEXIAO, C. (1988) Definitions and sciences of information. Information Processing & Management, v. 24, n. 4, p. 479-491.

ZEMAN, J. (1970) Philosophical meaning of the notion of information. In: The concept of information in contemporary science. Trad. Maria Helena Kühner. Rio de Janeiro: Peace and Earth.

"Writing technology books is much more than conveying information. It's about translating complexity into accessible language, sparking curiosity, and fostering understanding. As a writer in this field, I have the privilege of unraveling the mysteries of technology and inspiring others to explore the endless possibilities that technology offers us. It's a real dive into the future, sharing knowledge and building bridges between the world of innovation and the avid reader for discovery."

Prof. Marcão

12 MEET THE AUTHOR.

12.1 Prof. Marcão - Marcus Vinícius Pinto.

Figure 21 – Prof. Marcão and his platforms.

In my career, which has been marked by decades of experience in information technology and marketing, it is important to highlight my constant search for improvement and a deep understanding of information science and the complex functioning of the human mind.

Despite the challenge of living with a physical disability, more specifically the absence of the left foot, this singular fact has driven me to constantly seek to overcome and value the uniqueness of each individual.

Currently, I'm in a moment of consolidation in my career as a writer. I am deeply involved with topics related to information science and seek to bring to light an insightful and comprehensive view of the complex processes of data storage, organization, and dissemination.

Through my words, I seek to unveil the complexities of the human being and his mind in all its nuances.

During these decades, I have dedicated myself intensively to information architecture, attribute engineering and software development projects, using different methodologies to ensure the efficiency and quality of the products I am proud to create.

I understand the importance of proposing methodologies that allow optimizing resources and improving the quality of database projects. In this sense, I highlight the data modeling and Data Warehouse standards, as well as the methodology for validating and managing data models, which are fundamental to achieve solid and reliable results.

In addition to acting as a business consultant, where I offer innovative solutions to complex problems and help organizations overcome challenges, I am also dedicated to sharing my knowledge through lectures, training, and mentoring of careers and business development.

At the same time, I am a content producer on YouTube, which allows me to disseminate ideas and dialogue with an audience eager for knowledge and innovation.

Throughout my career, I have had the privilege of publishing 32 books to date, all of which are available on Amazon's platform, providing access to a wide audience in search of in-depth knowledge and insights.

However, even though I am involved in all these professional activities, I never let go of my constant learning process, finding happiness in the little things and pursuing my true purposes of helping those who seek me.

I have a deep respect for everyone and dedicate myself to activities that transcend work, such as the study of the universe of music on the piano.

In addition, my personal life is also important to me. I have been married to my beloved wife, Andrea, since 1998, and our union is filled with happiness and companionship.

12.2   Some books published by Prof. Marcão.

Figure 22– Some books by Prof. Marcão.

12.3 Books on Open Data by Prof. Marcão.

Figure 23 - Books on Open Data by Prof. Marcão.

12.4   How to contact Prof. Marcão.

For lectures, training and business mentoring, please contact me on my LinkedIn profile or by email marcao.tecno@gmail.com.

It will be a pleasure to interact with you.

Prof. Marcão – MARCUS VINÍCIUS PINTO

CONSULTING | MENTORING | TRAINING | LECTURES

marcao.tecno@gmail.com

https://bit.ly/linkedin_profmarcao

Be my follower and get access to unmissable content!

Instagram: https://bit.ly/3tpZ5kp

YouTube: https://bit.ly/4ah44nT

Linkedin: https://bit.ly/linkedin_profmarcao

My Amazon Author Page: https://amzn.to/3S2xCgL

Spotify: https://spoti.fi/3c0fClN

Linktree: https://linktr.ee/tudo_prof.marcao

MY CONSULTING FIRM: https://mvpconsult.com.br/

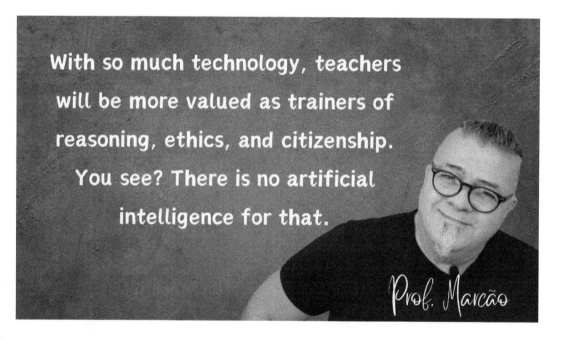

Figure 24 – Let's value teachers.

www.ingramcontent.com/pod-product-compliance
Lightning Source LLC
Chambersburg PA
CBHW080533060326
40690CB00022B/5112